UNBOUND

The Conscience of a Republican Delegate

CURLY HAUGLAND
& SEAN PARNELL

Citizens in Charge Foundation
Woodbridge, Virginia
www.CitizensinChargeFoundation.org

Citizens in Charge Foundation
13168 Centerpointe Way, Suite 202
Woodbridge, Virginia 22193
www.CitizensinChargeFoundation.org

ISBN-13: 978-1533411280
ISBN-10: 153341128X

Table of Contents

Preface

It is no exaggeration to say that the Republican Party was founded as the party of freedom. A collection of the official proceedings of the first three Republican National Conventions, compiled and published at the urging of the party in 1892, includes the following platform statement from the newly formed Republican Association of Washington, District of Columbia, in June 1855:

> Whereas, by the repeal of the eighth section of the act for the admission of Missouri into the Union, the Territories of Kansas and Nebraska have been opened to the introduction of slavery, and all the compromises, real or imaginary, upon that subject are thus violated and annulled, and deep dishonor inflicted upon the age in which we live:

> Now, therefore, in cooperation with all those throughout the land who oppose this and other similar measures, which deem to be contrary to the spirit of the Constitution, and which are designed to extend and perpetuate slavery, we do associate ourselves together under the name and title of THE REPUBLICAN ASSOCIATION OF WASHINGTON, D.C.[1]

While the battle against slavery was the most foundational and celebrated of the Republican Party's early principles, there was yet another principle of freedom that was central to the party as well – that individuals ought to have, in all matters before them at the convention, the freedom to vote their conscience and have that vote truly recorded and counted.

As this book demonstrates, this principle has been embedded within the rules of the party established at the first national nominating convention[2] held in Philadelphia, Pennsylvania, in 1856, recognizing that each and every delegate to the national convention had a full and unfettered right to vote as he wished on matters ranging from approval of rules, credential challenges, whether to uphold or overturn rulings of the chair,

and perhaps most importantly, on the nomination of the Republican Party's candidate for president and vice president of the United States.

This will likely come as a surprise to many, accustomed to hearing that delegates to the convention are allocated to one candidate or another based on the results of a primary, caucus, or other event, or media counts of how many delegates are officially bound to vote for a specific candidate at the convention, or speculation on how delegates might vote if a second ballot or even more are required to select a nominee.

But as this book makes clear, delegates to the Republican National Convention have had, at every convention from 1856 through 2012, the full freedom to vote their consciences on all matters recognized and protected in the convention rules – with the single notable exception of 1976, when the campaign of incumbent President Gerald Ford pushed through a change in the rules as part of a strategy to deny the nomination to former California Gov. Ronald Reagan.

This conclusion is based on a careful historical analysis of the official records of the Republican National Convention and Republican National Committee, such as rules committee meeting transcripts and the official proceedings, as well as academic research and contemporaneous media accounts. As documented here, both the rules and rulings from the convention chair on the matter have consistently upheld this right, and the statements of delegates and rules committee members consistently state the purpose of what are now Rule 37 (b) and 38, which is to preserve and protect the freedom of delegates to vote their consciences in all matters.

This finding is important at this time because additions to the rules in recent years – adopted either at the Republican National Convention or by the Republican National Committee – appear to conflict with this longstanding principle. As this book will document and explain, so long as the 2016 Republican National Convention adopts as standing rules for the convention what are now the temporary rules, or at least does not substantially change Rule 37 (b) and Rule 38, then the freedom of delegates to vote their conscience will be preserved.

But it is clear, based on recent developments, that there is at the very least a serious misunderstanding by many about the freedom of delegates to vote their consciences, and perhaps even a deliberate effort to strip away this important and longstanding freedom. Delegates to the 2016

convention ought to become familiar with the history of this freedom, and then judge for themselves whether they should fight to protect it or join in an effort to diminish it.

This book lays out the case for the proposition that, historically and necessarily, all delegates to the Republican National Convention have enjoyed the complete freedom to vote their consciences on all matters, including the nomination for president of the United States, with the exception of the 1976 convention.

Chapter 1 traces the origin and enforcement of this right from the first Republican National Convention in 1856 through the 1964 convention, when the rule addressing delegates' right to vote their consciences was clarified and strengthened.

Chapter 2 describes the events of the 1976 national convention, when the Ford campaign engineered a limitation on this longstanding right, and the 1980 convention, when the rules were restored to their pre-1976 language and the right was again recognized and fully protected under the rules.

Chapter 3 explains how, beginning with the 2000 convention and continuing on through a 2013 meeting of the Republican National Committee, the form and later the text of the rules governing the party were both subtly and then explicitly changed in ways that ostensibly strip away each delegate's freedom to vote his or her conscience. This chapter also explains why these changes to the rules ultimately cannot infringe or limit delegates' freedom to vote according to their own consciences.

Chapter 4 examines the longstanding understanding that national party rules trump state party rules whenever there is a conflict between the two, and documents the extensive legal history that prevents state legislators from interfering with the internal business of national political parties, such as by attempting to bind delegates to the result of any primary, caucus, convention, or any other contest.

Chapter 5 makes the argument that these protections for delegates' freedom to vote their consciences are a necessary and positive aspect of the political process and the freedom of the Republican Party to avoid government intrusion into its internal matters.

Chapter 6 recognizes that the position asserted here (that delegates to the Republican National Convention are "unbound" and free to vote their

consciences on all matters including the presidential nomination) is not universally held, and it attempts to address some of the critiques and objections that have been raised by those who disagree with the assertions and conclusions reached in this book.

Chapter 7 ends with the co-authors' thoughts and conclusions on the conscience protections embedded in the Republican National Convention's rules, and what it means in 2016 and beyond.

Every American enjoys the right to vote his or her conscience in all matters. This includes not only votes for public officials, like a mayor or senator, but in private associations as well, such as when electing the head of a neighborhood association. This right is integral to the nation's identity as a democratic republic, where legitimate power derives from the people's free choices in the voting booth, based on their own intrinsic sets of judgments, priorities and preferences. As this book proves, delegates to the Republican National Convention are no different from any American asked to cast a vote on matters large or small – they retain the freedom to vote their consciences, and no rule or law can or ought to bind them against their better judgment.

---

[1] Proceedings of the First Three Republican National Conventions. (1893). 2.

[2] Technically the first convention was held in Pittsburgh, Pennsylvania, in February 1856, but did not engage in any nominating activity. That convention appointed a committee to call for a national convention to nominate candidates for president and vice president, which was convened in Philadelphia in June of 1856.

Chapter 1 –
History of the "Unit Rule"

"There never was a convention, there never can be a convention, of
which I am one delegate, equal in rights to every other delegate,
that shall bind my vote against my will on any question whatever."

– James A. Garfield at the 1880 Republican convention[1]

In 1880, the Republican National Committee gathered in Chicago to
choose its nominee for president. The leading contenders were James
Blaine, U.S. senator from Maine; former President Ulysses S. Grant; and
Secretary of the Treasury John Sherman.

The nomination would eventually go to James Garfield, at the time a
sitting congressman and senator-elect from Ohio who had come to Chicago to manage the effort to nominate Sherman. He had placed Sherman's
name into nomination, and also served as chairman of the rules committee
at the convention. After 35 deadlocked roll calls, none of the contenders
succeeded in getting a majority of delegates. Garfield emerged as a
compromise choice on the 36th ballot and was elected president later that
year.

The question of who should be the Republican nominee wasn't the
only hotly contested issue, however. One of the other key issues was
whether something known as the "unit rule" would be in effect for the
Republican convention, a seemingly arcane and technical issue but one of
vital importance. Had the 1880 GOP convention allowed the unit rule, it is
quite possible that Grant, not Garfield, would have been the Republican
nominee. While historians and others could debate endlessly what might
have been with Grant as the 1880 nominee instead of Garfield, this
chapter will focus on a simple question: What is the unit rule and why is it
so important?

Broadly speaking, a unit rule in the context of a national political
convention requires that all the delegates' votes from a state be awarded
based on how a majority of the delegation votes. So if a state has 40

delegates to the convention, and 30 support Candidate A while 10 support Candidate B, then the votes of all 40 delegates will be awarded to Candidate A if a unit rule is in effect.

In and of itself, the unit rule was not what these early Republican conventions found objectionable. Rather – as the debate, discussion, and rules adopted by the party in this time period make clear – procedures to eliminate any use of the unit rule were in service of the principle that every single delegate arriving at the Republican convention was free to vote according to his conscience, regardless of any instructions or pledges imposed by the state party or others.

The unit rule traces back to the 1832 Democratic convention,[2] the second convention held by any major party in U.S. history (the National Republicans, headed by Henry Clay of Kentucky, held the first, in December 1831). There the Democratic party adopted a rule stating "[t]hat in taking the vote the majority of delegates from each state designate the person by whom the votes for that state shall be given."[3]

Although ambiguous to the modern ear, this rule gave the majority of a delegation the authority to cast all of a state's votes for a single candidate, even if one or more delegates preferred another candidate.

Although the unit rule was first established in that 1832 convention, not until the second Democratic convention in 1835 did it appear to face a challenge, when an Ohio delegate protested the awarding of all 21 delegate votes from the state to Richard M. Johnson as the vice presidential nominee because the delegation's vote hadn't been unanimous. The chair of the convention upheld the vote tally announced by the delegation chair, and all 21 votes were recorded for Johnson.[4]

The Democratic Party convention in 1848 went even further, adopting a rule specifying that in announcing vote totals, "the manner in which said vote is cast to be decided by the delegation of each state for itself." This rule further entrenched the unit rule giving the majority of each state's delegation the power to compel the minority's votes be awarded against its wishes. The issue was perhaps most forcefully settled at the 1852 convention, which finally decided on the 49th ballot to nominate Franklin Pierce for president.

On the 20th ballot of that convention, the Virginia delegation's chairman cast all 15 of its votes for James Buchanan, one of the leading

contenders for the Democratic nomination that year. The Virginia delega-tion then briefly left the convention hall for "consultation," as the official proceedings described it. Upon their return, the chairman of the delegation described the rules of the state party, which he said bound him to cast all 15 of the state's ballots for Buchanan. At this point another delegate, Virginia Gov. John Floyd, rose and announced his dissension from the announced vote total, saying to the convention president the following:

> When I came to this Convention, upon the first organization of the
> Virginia delegation, I subscribed to the usage of the party, with a
> protest against the right of that delegation to prescribe a rule or to
> dictate a law.... I am and have been perfectly willing to go with the
> rest of the Virginia delegation, for the purpose of securing to her
> that moral power which we are all there so proud of. But, sir, when
> the time has arrived when the action of Virginia is no longer
> efficacious, I, as the representative of ten thousand freemen, protest
> against being dragged along at the car of any man. I therefore, on
> my own behalf, and under the instructions of my colleagues, cast
> the vote of the 13th Congressional district of Virginia for Stephen
> A. Douglas of Illinois.... I am compelled to assume before this
> Convention, of asking that they should accord to the 13th district of
> the Democracy of Virginia the privilege which is exercised by every
> other district throughout the wide-spread boundaries of the United
> States – the privilege of voting for the man they prefer.[5]

Following Floyd's comments, the convention president read the relevant rule allowing the majority to cast all of the delegation's votes for a single candidate, and another Virginia delegate (identified only as Mr. Wise) argued against Floyd's position. After several motions and rulings from the chair, yet another Virginia delegate, identified as N.C. Claiborne, offered the following in response:

> When we entered this Convention, three of the districts of Virginia
> were for one individual, three were for another, one stood tied
> between two of the contending candidates, and there was a bare
> majority of one for the gentleman for whom Virginia has thus far

> cast her vote. The six districts which are in favor for the other candidates contain a majority of more than 20,000 of the Democracy of Virginia. And are we to be told that voice is to be stifled, because the Democratic Convention of the State of Virginia recommended to the delegation to Baltimore to cast the vote of the state as a unit by a majority of the districts?[6]

Following the statement by Claiborne, the convention president announced that all 15 of Virginia's votes would be recorded as cast for Buchanan, in line with the unit rule. A similar protest was later lodged by a member of the Georgia delegation during the 35th ballot,[7] when the state's delegation gave its 10 votes to Douglas after having supported Buchanan on the 34 preceding ballots.[8] This protest was ignored.

The 1860 Democratic convention added language to the rule clarifying that delegations without such instructions were free to vote according to their consciences, again recognizing that, in the Democratic Party, states had the authority to bind delegates on how to vote:

> That in any state which has not provided or directed by its state convention how its vote may be given, the convention will recognize the right of each delegate to cast his individual vote.[9]

The unit rule continued to be a part of the Democratic nomination process until 1968, when the convention voted to release all delegates from the rule.[10] But during that time it continued to draw criticism – including this from Franklin D. Roosevelt in 1920, who would go on to be the party's vice presidential nominee that year and 12 years later be elected president:

> Let the people feel that the Democratic choice was made in a real Democratic way, by a free and frank interchange of opinion among the delegates with every man voting according to his conscience, and we will have, in my judgment, a tremendous advantage at the very start of the campaign.[11]

Following the 1968 convention, the Democrats established the Commission on Party Structure and Delegate Selection, more frequently known as the McGovern-Fraser Commission after the two men who chaired it, and based on its recommendations the Democratic Party eliminated the unit rule altogether ahead of the 1972 convention.[12]

While the Democrats had more than 130 years of binding delegates to vote according to a delegation's majority or the directions of the state party, the Republican Party rejected binding delegates from the outset.

The first GOP convention was held in Philadelphia in 1856. The Republican Party largely rose from the remnants of the Whig Party, which had fallen apart over the issue of slavery and its expansion into Western territories. At that first convention former Army officer and California Gov. John Fremont won the nomination on the first ballot, defeating Judge John McLean of Ohio.

The rules for the convention laid out a process that was designed to ensure that each delegate to the convention was free to vote for the candidate of his choice, and most importantly, have that vote recognized in the official tally. This may have at least in part been driven by the experience of watching the Democratic Party's practice of forcing its delegates to vote against their individual consciences on party business, including nominations.

The rule adopted at that first convention was as follows:

> That in voting for a candidate for President, the states be called in their order, and that the chairman of each delegation present the number of votes given to each candidate for President by the delegates from his state...[13]

Reading the rule from that first convention closely, it is clear that it is the duty of the delegation's chair to accurately and honestly report how delegates *actually* voted, as opposed to some modification or limitation imposed on delegates by custom or the instructions of the party back home, or the wishes of a majority of delegates.

While it might seem a stretch to read that much into what on its face seems a relatively simple rule, the comments described in the official proceedings of James W. Webb of the New York delegation, a staunch ally

of William H. Seward's bid for the Republican nomination, indicate the prevailing view regarding each delegate's duty to exercise his own judgment in determining for whom to vote:

> The same great cause, be he who he may, who was to carry their banner, was dear to the heart of every man here. [Cheers.] Undoubtedly they had come to this Convention to express their judgements in the earnest way that their feelings or their convictions may have prompted. And he for one felt that he had discharged his duty to his constituents and he was willing to accord every man that he, too, had according to the best of his judgement, discharged what he deemed to be his duty to his constituents and his duty to his country.[14]

This expectation of each delegate being free to vote his own conscience on matters before the convention can be seen in the vice presidential nomination for the new party. Among the leading contenders were William L. Dayton, former U.S. senator from New Jersey, and a former congressman from Illinois named Abraham Lincoln. An informal poll of the delegates showed Dayton far and away would be the winner, and most of the other contenders asked to have their names withdrawn, seeing that they would not be nominated. Dayton won an overwhelming majority, with Lincoln and a few other drawing a smattering of votes.

As was customary in those days, a new roll call vote was requested with the aim of making the vote unanimous, and a delegate from Illinois rose to ask those who had previously voted for Lincoln to now vote for Dayton. Unanimous state delegation votes rolled in until Pennsylvania's vote was called for:

> Dr. Gazzam, of Western Pennsylvania, rose to ask to have the vote of Pennsylvania recorded unanimously for William L. Dayton. But he was informed that one delegate had not yet made up his mind....

> Wm. S. Pierce, Esq., the only dissenting Pennsylvania delegate, rose and withdrew his dissent.[15]

The question of whether Republican delegates were considered free to vote their consciences, regardless of any instructions from the state party or the delegation's majority, was more directly addressed at the 1860 convention, the first time a state party chair is known to have attempted to report the delegation's votes based on something other than the actual votes of the delegates. The primary contenders for the Republican nomination that year were Lincoln, former Rep. Edward Bates of Missouri, Sen. Simon Cameron of Pennsylvania, Gov. Salmon Chase of Ohio, and Sen. William Seward of New York.

The 1860 rule was different than that of the previous convention, though the practice and intent was identical:

> Four votes shall be cast by the delegates at large of each state and each congressional district shall be entitled to two votes. The votes of each delegation shall be reported by its chairman.[16]

At that convention, the expectation that each delegate would be allowed to cast his vote according to his own conscience was first tested. On the first ballot the Maryland delegation's chair, a Mr. Cochrane, made the following statement in announcing his delegation's vote:

> The Republican State Convention of Maryland having requested that the delegation should vote as a unit, I therefore, in accordance with the wishes of a majority of the delegation, cast 11 votes for Edward Bates.[17]

This was immediately protested by Mr. Coale, a Maryland delegate, whose comments included the following:

> I object to that. I am a freeman in Maryland … we were not instructed, and that we will not act according to the recommendation except insofar as we please.

Whereupon another Maryland delegate, Mr. Armour, rose and explained that the Maryland convention had rejected binding the delegates

and instead opted merely to recommend they vote as a unit, and added the following:

> Not one of us considered that the recommendation was equivalent to an instruction. Therefore ... believing then and now that we were free to cast our votes for the man of our choice, and we now claim that right on the floor of the Convention.

To which Coale added:

> We will vote as we please, and we will not vote in any other way.

During further discussion of the point, the convention chair noted that the rule stated "that the vote of each State should be announced by its Chairman." An unidentified delegate immediately offered a clarification: "He must but announce it and announce it truly."

> **"We will vote as we please, and we will not vote in any other way."**

The issue was put to a vote of the convention as a whole, and while the vote totals were not recorded, the decision was to reject the Maryland chair's attempt to impose the unit rule.[18] Maryland's vote was recorded on the first ballot with eight delegates voting for Bates, and three for Seward.[19]

The 1860 decision is not decisively and unequivocally in favor of the right of delegates to be free to vote as they please without regard to instructions from the state convention or other authority, as part of the issue involved related to whether the Maryland convention had issued an "instruction" or merely a "recommendation." Later conventions, however, settled the issue more conclusively, and affirmed the right of delegates to, as Mr. Coale put it, "vote as we please."

At the 1868 convention, former Union Gen. Grant was unanimously nominated, and the unanimity does not appear to have been artificially manufactured or contrived – he was the only candidate nominated on the convention floor, and he was wildly popular among Republicans and the general public as well (at least outside the South).

There are strong indications in the official proceedings of the 1868 convention that several delegations arrived with instructions from state conventions to vote for Grant, such as the Missouri delegation chair's statement that "the State Convention of Missouri instructed the delegation to vote for Ulysses S. Grant .... Missouri gives General Grant twenty-two votes,"[20] and New Jersey's delegation chair said in announcing his state's vote, "[T]he New Jersey delegation, instructed by her Convention – and in giving these instructions, she spoke the voice of every man of the Republican party within her borders – now delivers their fourteen votes for Ulysses S. Grant."[21] No delegates rose to challenge these announced votes, however, and Grant unquestionably was the runaway favorite – no other candidate was even placed in nomination.

But the vice-presidential nomination was not so easily settled. Eleven candidates, including Gov. Andrew Curtin of Pennsylvania, received votes from delegates. The delegation from Pennsylvania arrived at the convention with instructions to vote as a unit for Curtin's nomination, but four delegates dissented and wanted to vote for other candidates.[22] The convention upheld their freedom to vote their consciences,[23] and their votes were recorded for Speaker of the House Schuyler Colfax of Indiana (1) and Sen. Benjamin Wade of Ohio (3).

The definitive test of whether delegates to the Republican National Convention could be bound and have their votes announced contrary to their wishes occurred in 1876, when the Pennsylvania delegation again arrived with instructions from its state party to vote as a single unit for their current governor, John Hartranft.[24]

By this time, the Republican convention had two separate rules addressing the matter of how votes were to be announced and recorded:

Rule 2: Each state shall be entitled to double the number of its senators and representatives in congress, according to the late apportionment, and each territory and the District of Columbia shall be entitled to two votes. The votes of each delegation shall be reported by its chairman.

Rule 6: In the record of votes by states, the vote of each state, territory, and the District of Columbia shall be announced by the

chairman; and, in case the vote of any state, territory, or the District of Columbia shall be divided, the chairman shall announce the number of votes cast for any candidate, or for or against any proposition.[25]

The question of binding delegates was hotly debated on the floor of the convention. On the first ballot, Pennsylvania cast all 58 of its votes for Hartranft, with no objection from any delegate. On the second ballot, however, when the chair of the Pennsylvania delegation again announced that all 58 votes had been cast for Hartranft, one of the delegates objected with the following statement:

> The vote for Pennsylvania was not correctly announced: myself and my colleague, representing the Sixth Congressional District ... wish to cast our votes for James G. Blaine. We requested the chairman of the delegation to so announce our votes, but he refused, and we now ask and demand that our votes shall be recorded for James G. Blaine.[26]

According to the official proceedings, two more Pennsylvania delegates also requested that their votes be recorded for Blaine. The president of the convention quickly offered his ruling:

> The gentleman ... rise[s] to a point of order, which is that the report of the vote made by the chairman of the delegation is not the report of the vote cast in the delegation, which, of course, raises a question of the very highest privilege. That point of order being raised, the chair rules that it is the right of any and every member equally, to vote his sentiments in the convention.[27]

Following the convention president's ruling, the chair of the Pennsylvania delegation appealed to the entire convention, and what followed was an extensive debate, including two voice votes and two roll call votes. Of the 115 pages documenting the official proceedings of a three-day convention, 13 pages are consumed with this single matter.

Passionate arguments both for and against the right of delegates to vote freely were delivered. Speaking forcefully in favor of allowing delegates to vote according to their own consciences, a Mr. Ingersoll of Illinois made the following remarks:

> The simple question before this convention is, whether each delegate has a right to vote as he believes the people he represents wish him to vote, or whether he can be tied by packed caucuses, whether he can be tied by party machinery, and forced to vote against the sentiments of his constituents and against his own choice. I tell you that we cannot afford to go to this country upon the idea that a delegate from a state can be forced, against his will and against his conscience, to vote for a man that he does not believe his constituents want. It has been decided by a Republican convention for the United States, and it was decided in the case of Pennsylvania, that, notwithstanding an instruction to vote as a unit the delegates had a right to vote as they pleased.... For one I believe in allowing every delegate upon this floor the right to vote his choice, the right to represent his constituents.[28]

Ingersoll's view was not uncontested, as immediately after he spoke a delegate from Indiana, Mr. Thompson, rose in defense of the unit rule:

> The simple question to be now decided by the is convention is this: whether, after we have been sent here by our state conventions, under instructions from them, we have the individual right to violate those instructions; whether the voice of a sovereign state, declared through her state authorities, shall be defied by individuals under claim of a personal right.... When [the dissenting Pennsylvania delegates] accepted their position as members of this convention, they became bound by every consideration of justice, of right, of truth, and of honor, to obey those instructions.[29]

A Mr. Woodford of New York weighed in as well, offering the following comments:

> I believe that under the very existence alike of the nation and the Republican party, is the right of every man to cast his own vote … As an honorable man I am bound, as honorable men you are bound, to abide the actions of the convention; but should this or any convention make a declaration of unworthy principles, or place thereon candidates whose lives and records to not represent what true Republicanism means, then let me to-day and here simply say, in words so plain that none may misunderstand, I am bound to my country and its welfare by a higher tie than that which binds me to the Republican party.[30]

After these and several other delegates spoke, the final roll call on the question was 395 to uphold the convention president's decision, 353 against. The president of the convention summarized the decision with the following words: "[I]t is the right of every individual member thereof to vote his individual sentiments."[31]

With that Pennsylvania's vote on the second ballot was officially recorded as 54 for Hartranft and four for Blaine, and a third ballot was called (Rutherford B. Hayes, former governor of Ohio, eventually won the nomination on the seventh ballot).

"[I]t is the right of every individual member thereof to vote his individual sentiments."

Once again the principle that delegates could not be bound to specific candidates, or at least that the Republican National Convention would not accept such binding, had survived another convention.

The next convention, held in Chicago in 1880, saw the last serious effort to bind delegates until 1976. Former President Grant was seeking to be re-nominated for a third term, and his allies led delegations from Illinois, New York, and Pennsylvania. These were then, as now, populous states that could help tip the nomination towards their favored candidate, particularly if all the delegate votes were announced for him. Both the New York and Pennsylvania delegations were instructed by their state conventions to cast their votes unanimously, and the Illinois delegation was selected through a controversial change in procedures that also

produced a pro-Grant delegation.[32] Delegates from Alabama, Arkansas, Kentucky and Texas had been ordered to vote for Grant as well.[33]

The key to getting all of these delegates' votes recorded for Grant was getting a pro-Grant convention chairman, who would rule that state delegations arriving with unit rule instructions from their state conventions were bound to cast all votes according to the majority's wishes.[34] But instead, the Republican National Committee met beforehand and the anti-Grant majority there proposed the following resolution:

> *Resolved*, that the committee recognize the right of each delegate in a Republican National Convention freely to cast and to have counted his individual vote therein according to his own senti- ments, and, if he so decide, against any unit rule or other instruc- tions passed by a state convention; which right was conceded without dissent and was exercised in the conventions of 1860 and 1868, and was after full debate confirmed by the convention of 1876; and has thus become a part of the law of Republican Conven- tions and until reversed by a convention itself must remain a governing principle.[35]

The chair of the national committee, Sen. Don Cameron of Pennsylvania, was a Grant ally, and he did all he could to prevent the measure from passing because it would effectively end the attempt to enforce the unit rule. Finally, with his chairmanship at risk, he relented, and though the resolution did not pass, it was agreed that the unit rule would not be enforced in the temporary convention, and Garfield, at the time a congressman from Ohio, would be named the rules committee chair.[36]

Shortly after arriving in Chicago, Garfield was approached by a reporter from *The Chicago Tribune* and asked his position on the unit rule. His response left little ambiguity on his stance:

> [A]ll delegates … are political units, each one of whom has a right to express his own political sentiments by his own personal vote.… It is wholly un-Republican for one man to cast another man's vote.[37]

In line with these sentiments, Garfield crafted what was then Rule 8 of the convention:

> In the record of the vote by States, the vote of each State, territory, and the District of Columbia shall be announced by the chairman; and in case the vote of any State, territory, or District of Columbia shall be divided, the chairman shall announce the number of votes cast for any candidate, or for or against any proposition; but if exception is taken by any delegate to the correctness of such announcement by the chairman of his delegation, the President of the Convention shall direct the roll of members of such delegation to be called, and the result shall be recorded with the votes individually given.[38]

This rule finally added what had been lacking in previous conventions – a specified procedure that would effectively forestall the unit rule or any other effort to bind delegates' votes.

The Grant forces appear to have made a last-ditch effort to force an early vote on the nomination before the rules were adopted, presumably thinking that some delegates might still feel bound by instructions from or pledges to their state parties without Rule 8 in place. Garfield argued that the rules be voted on first, and included the following statement:

> Settle the rule. Settle it in any way you please. Make it the unit rule and I am bound by it. Make it the individual rule – that each individual shall have the right to vote – and I am bound by it, for two great reasons: first, because you make it the rule, and greater still, because I believe it to be an everlasting right.[39]

Following further discussion, the convention adopted the rules proposed by Garfield and the rules committee. But even before the incorporation of this specific language into the rules, the principle of each delegate being able to vote freely was upheld on multiple occasions at the 1880 convention. The roll call vote on a motion to require the credentials committee to report before the rules committee includes the following exchange:

Upon the call of the State of Alabama:

Mr. TURNER, of Alabama. Alabama votes twenty aye.

Mr. ALEXANDER, of Alabama. I desire to vote no.

The PRESIDENT. Does the gentleman from Alabama desire that his vote should be received in the negative?

Mr. ALEXANDER. Yes, sir.

Mr. PRESIDENT. It will be so recorded.

Mr. ALEXANDER. I desire to explain, sir.

Mr. PRESIDENT. No explanation is in order.[40]

The Kentucky delegation had a similar moment, after the delegation chair announced its vote on the same question, "Under instructions from the convention of the State of Kentucky, Kentucky casts twenty-four votes aye." A delegate rose to challenge the vote as announced, and said a total of four delegates wished to vote "no." Seeing that the convention chair was prepared to accept the dissenting votes, the Alabama delegation chair announced a new vote total: 20 aye, four no.[41]

During the 36 ballots it took the convention to eventually choose Garfield, nearly every delegation arriving with instructions to vote as a unit ignored them. On the first ballot, for example, New York split its 70 delegate votes between Grant (51), Blaine (17) and Sherman (2), while Pennsylvania cast its 58 votes for a combination of Grant (32), Blaine (23) and Sherman (3) as well. Alabama, Illinois, Kentucky and Texas all ignored their instructions from home, while only Arkansas continued to cast all 12 delegate votes for Grant throughout the convention, and without challenge from any member of the delegation.[42]

Rule 8 was invoked several times during the 36 ballots. On the second ballot, the Florida delegation chair announced the state's eight votes had been cast for Grant (identical to how the delegation voted on the first

ballot), but one of the delegates announced he had voted for Blaine and wanted his vote recorded as such. Using the new rule, the president of the convention polled the delegation and announced the result as seven for Grant, one for Blaine.[43]

The balance of the occasions when Rule 8 was invoked appear to have been in response to simple errors in the vote announcement by delegation chairs – the Virginia chair, for example, attempted to cast 16 votes for Grant, two for Blaine, four for Sherman, and one for Garfield, totaling 23 votes. The problem was that Virginia only had 22 votes. Upon the poll of the delegates, it was found that the chair had been in error and only 15 votes had been cast for Grant.[44]

While a seemingly trivial error, the fact that the convention chair used the procedure of Rule 8 on this occasion and others where simple mistakes appear to have been made demonstrates the point that the rule was not exclusively for deterring the unit rule from being used. Instead, it was put in place to ensure that the individual vote of each delegate would be recorded accurately and according to his or her own judgment and conscience.

The rule that was adopted by the 1880 convention remained largely unchanged for the next several decades. At the 1884 convention, delegations were polled on 37 occasions, most of them during the vote on the presidential nominee.

One instance it was *not* invoked demonstrates the point that it was entirely the responsibility of a delegate to challenge a vote cast against his conscience – absent such a challenge, the delegation chair is able to announce the vote according to a unit rule or other instruction from the state party, and the vote will be recorded as announced. On the third ballot at the 1884 convention, the proceedings recorded the following regarding Georgia's announcement:

> Mr. BUCK, the Chairman of that delegation, said: By instructions of my delegation before coming into this convention, we agreed to act as a unit. A majority of the delegation are still for Chester A. Arthur, and unless a vote is called, I shall so announce. Twenty-four votes for Arthur.

The PRESIDENT. Is there any contest in Georgia?

SEVERAL DELEGATES. No, no.[45]

With no delegate willing to stand up to challenge the announced vote, the roll call proceeded to the next state.

The following convention in 1888 saw 31 separate invocations of the conscience protections, almost all of them during the balloting on the presidential nominee. Further evidence that the Garfield language was aimed at any effort to deny delegates the right to vote their conscience (including but not limited to the unit rule) can be seen in the following fact: In 49 out of the 68 occasions when the language was invoked at the 1884 and 1888 conventions, the initial vote announcement was not unanimous but was split between different candidates or propositions.

The procedure crafted by Garfield and adopted as Rule 8 at the 1880 convention continued to be invoked on a regular basis over the next several decades. In one of the more bizarre instances recorded, at the 1892 convention the Ohio delegation voted overwhelmingly for their governor, William McKinley, who was not seeking the presidency. Not only was McKinley not a candidate, he was the convention chair that year, and as soon as the Ohio vote was announced he challenged it and ordered a poll of the delegation. The delegation chair said McKinley could not challenge the count because he was no longer a delegate from Ohio and that his place had been taken by an alternate when he became convention chair. McKinley ruled he was still a delegate entitled to challenge the announced vote and ordered a poll, which revealed nearly every delegate had in fact voted for him.[46]

The 1912 convention fight between incumbent President William Taft and former President Theodore Roosevelt was hotly contested, and during a roll call vote relating to disputed credentials, delegates from multiple states stood up to challenge the announced vote totals, including those from Arkansas, California, Georgia, Indiana, Kentucky, New York, North Carolina, Oregon, Pennsylvania and Texas. In several cases the polling of the delegates revealed different vote totals than those originally announced, and the polling ensured delegates' true preferences were recorded.[47]

The North Carolina challenge was particularly illustrative in terms of the conscience protections afforded Republican delegates. The convention proceedings record the following:

> MR. RICHMOND PEARSON, of North Carolina (when North Carolina was called). – As chairman of the North Carolina delegation, I have been instructed by resolution to cast the vote of North Carolina 23 to 1 in favor of Roosevelt on all motions preliminary to the ballot for the nomination for President. I therefore announce the vote of North Carolina in accordance with that resolution, 1 yea and 23 nay.

> MR. JOHN C. MATTHEWS, of North Carolina. – Mr. Chairman, the chairman of the North Carolina delegation announced 1 vote yeah, which was from the First district. I am from the Fourth district, and I also desire to be recorded "Yea."

> THE TEMPORARY CHAIRMAN. – Does the gentleman challenge the vote of North Carolina?

> MR. MATTHEWS, of North Carolina. – Yes.

> THE TEMPORARY CHAIRMAN. – Do you desire a roll call?

> MR. MATTHEWS, of North Carolina. – Yes.

> THE TEMPORARY CHAIRMAN. – The vote of North Carolina having been challenged, the Secretary will call the roll of that delegation.

> The Secretary called the roll of the North Carolina delegation, and the result was announced: Yeas, 2; nays, 22.[48]

On several additional roll calls, delegates challenged the results announced by the delegation chair, and in every single instance, the convention chair ordered a poll of the delegation be taken, with the votes

of each delegate accorded to his wishes.[49] The Illinois delegation arrived with instructions to cast its vote for Roosevelt,[50] but on the actual roll call for the presidential nomination, the Illinois delegation chair made the following statement:

> Mr. Chairman, it is impossible to get the exact vote of our State. A number of the delegates desire to have the vote challenged. I request that the roll of the Illinois delegation be called, with this preliminary statement: The great majority of our delegates feel that in view of the provisions of the primary law of our state, recently enacted, we have no power to cancel our instructions, and will vote for Theodore Roosevelt.[51]

The delegation was polled, with Roosevelt receiving 53, Taft two, and three absent or not voting.

When Oregon came up, the delegation's chair announced that the state's newly-enacted primary law required all ten delegates to cast their votes for Roosevelt, but two of them refused to do so, saying they wished to be recorded as "present and not voting." Another Oregon delegate asked the delegation be polled, and in the end the two non-voting delegates wishes were respected and their votes recorded as present and not voting while the other eight delegates voted for Roosevelt.[52]

The 1912 convention is the first example of a delegation citing, not instructions from their state party, but instructions based on a state law and the results of a primary election. Notably, in both instances the Illinois[53] and Oregon delegations' instructions were ignored, and the delegates' individual preferences were recorded instead.

The Republican Party's conscience protections were again invoked at the 1920 convention, including in one

> **The 1912 convention is the first example of a delegation citing... instructions based on a state law and the results of a primary election. Notably, in both instances... the instructions were ignored, and the delegates' individual preferences were recorded instead.**

instance by a delegate who was attempting to require the entire delegation to vote for the winner of the state's primary, Hiram Johnson, then a U.S. senator from California (he had also been the governor of California and was Theodore Roosevelt's running mate in 1912). As in 1912, Oregon's law purported to bind delegates to support the winner of the state primary.

The official proceedings documented what happened:

> MR. JOHN L. RAND, of Oregon (when Oregon was called, the vote having been announced as 9 for Johnson and 1 for Wood). – Mr. Chairman, I challenge the correctness of that vote. The primary held in the State of Oregon instructed us to vote for Hiram W. Johnson.

> THE PERMANENT CHAIRMAN. – You can ask for a poll of the delegation if you wish?

> MR. JOHN L. RAND, of Oregon. – Then I demand a poll of the Oregon delegation.

> THE PERMANENT CHAIRMAN. – The Secretary will call the roll of delegates for the State of Oregon and let each answer to his name.

> The Secretary for the Convention having called the roll of the Oregon delegation, the result was announced: Johnson 9, Wood 1...[54]

An Oregon delegate (he is not identified by name in the proceedings) similarly demanded a poll of the delegation on the third ballot after Johnson received eight votes to Wood's two, again citing "instructions" to the delegation to vote for Johnson, presumably meaning the state law binding them to support Johnson. The secretary again recorded the votes as given by each individual delegate, eight for Johnson and two for Wood.[55]

While the Oregon incident is interesting in reinforcing that the Republican National Convention historically had no regard for binding or requiring delegates to vote in accordance with primary results, the Michi-

gan episode in that same convention shows the conscience protections in full force.

On the first five ballots all 30 of Michigan's votes had been given to Johnson. On the sixth ballot, before the vote total could be announced, a delegate requested the delegation be polled, and the results showed 18 delegates continuing to vote for Johnson, 11 for Wood, and one for Lowden. The seventh ballot apparently shows why a poll of the delegation had been requested on the sixth ballot even before the results were announced – it appears the pro-Johnson delegates were attempting to misreport the vote, as the following exchange demonstrates:

> A DELEGATE FROM MICHIGAN. — Mr. Chairman, I challenge the announcement of the vote of Michigan as 30 for Johnson and ask for a poll of the delegation.

> THE PRESIDING OFFICER (MR. FREDERICK H. GILLETT, of Massachusetts). — The Secretary will poll the Michigan delegation in order that each individual delegate may announce his choice.

> The Secretary having resumed and concluded the roll call of the Michigan delegation, the vote was announced: Johnson, 10; Wood, 13; Lowden, 7.[56]

Michigan delegates again requested a poll of the delegation on the ninth ballot, presumably for similar reasons.[57] In addition on the ninth ballot Oklahoma's delegation chair announced all 20 votes for Harding, but a delegate requested a poll of the delegation and the results showed only 18 votes for Harding, with the other votes cast for two other candidates.[58] A Texas delegate also requested a roll call despite the opposition of many other delegates, prompting the convention chair to observe that "[a]ny member of any delegation has the right to demand a roll call."[59] The initial results of 22 votes for Warren G. Harding, then a U.S. senator from Ohio, and one for another candidate were changed as a result of the polling of the delegation to 19½ for Harding (fractional voting was allowed at the time) and the remainder for three other candidates or absent.[60]

In addition to these challenges, on the second ballot, delegates from Georgia and North Carolina also demanded polls of the delegation;[61] on the fifth ballot an Ohio delegate requested a poll;[62] on the sixth ballot delegation polls were requested from Georgia and Ohio;[63] on the seventh ballot Florida and Texas requested a poll;[64] and on the 10th (and final) ballot, won by Harding, Maryland requested a poll of the delegation.[65] In all cases the convention chair ordered the delegation to be polled and their votes recorded as announced. On the vice-presidential nomination, won overwhelmingly by Massachusetts Gov. Calvin Coolidge, a California delegate also requested a poll of the delegation, and received it.[66]

The language originally written by Garfield remained in the rules of the Republican National Convention largely without change until 1964, when the convention rules committee proposed new language specific to the unit rule, which would add the following to section (a) of what was then Rule 18, appending it to the longstanding language:

> No delegate or alternate shall be bound by any attempt of any state or Congressional District, the District of Columbia, Puerto Rico, or The Virgin Islands to impose the unit rule.[67]

The discussion in the rules committee focused largely on the fact that this was a clarification of longstanding policy. A Mr. Ross, who identifies himself in the transcript as the chairman of the subcommittee that recommended this addition, explained what was meant by the change. Citing the existing language written by Garfield, Ross said the following:

> Now that sentence in different language is and has been for a long time an effective method of preventing the imposition of the unit rule upon any delegate. All any delegate has to do is stand up and say, I want a poll of the delegation and his vote be recorded in accordance with his wishes regardless of any attempt on the part of any delegation either at a state convention, by state law, or by the state delegation to impose on him a position or person he does not wish to support.

Another delegate, identified in the transcript as Mr. Scribner, explained that the explicit prohibition on a unit rule was being added to provide clarity:

> The only reason that this sentence has been put in here is because we have had over the past two or three years from many members of this Committee, from interested Republicans, and more recently from people who are delegates, saying we are not lawyers and we don't understand all the implications and if the Republican Party doesn't have the unit rule, in other words a delegate coming to this Convention has the right to stand up and vote his judgement at the time, we'd like to have somebody say so.[68]

Another delegate, who was not identified but was from Oklahoma, then offered further information on the Republican Party's traditional view on the binding of delegates:

> In February, in Oklahoma, prior to our state convention, there was a great deal of discussion about an instructed delegation. I was familiar with the rule and attitude of the Republican Party at the National Convention and knew traditionally we had never honored instructed delegates or the unit rule.[69]

Following some further discussion, the amendment was voted on and, according to the transcript, passed unanimously. The explicit ban on a unit rule has remained in the GOP convention rules ever since.

As this history demonstrates, the longstanding ban on the unit rule is not, in fact, specifically about the rule itself. There are in fact understandable reasons for having such a rule and advantages to be had, as several scholars from The Brookings Institution described in 1964:

> A state party has undoubtedly often imposed a unit rule on its delegation to keep intact the greatest possible voting weight in the convention voting. When a delegation is allowed to divide its vote, part of the delegation merely cancels the other part. The state's

influence on the nominating decision is visibly reduced, and its bargaining position in national party councils weakened.[70]

But whatever real benefit there may have been in the past for such a rule, the Republican Party always rejected anything that might strip from individual delegates their right to vote according to their conscience on any and all matters that arise at the national convention. Until, that is, the 1976 battle between incumbent President Gerald Ford and his challenger for the GOP nomination, former California Gov. Ronald Reagan.

---

[1] Proceedings of the 1880 Republican National Convention, 40. Garfield was speaking on a resolution that would bind all delegates to the convention to support the party's eventual nominee, which had been offered by Grant ally Sen. Roscoe Conkling of New York.

[2] Becker, C. (1899). The Unit Rule in National Nominating Conventions. The American Historical Review, 5(1), 65. Republished online by Oxford University Press.

[3] Ibid.

[4] Ibid.

[5] Proceedings of the 1852 Democratic National Convention, 26.

[6] Ibid., 28.

[7] Ibid., 34.

[8] Ibid., 21-32.

[9] Proceedings of the 1860 Democratic National Convention, 10.

[10] Parris, J. (1973). The Convention Problem: Issues in reform of presidential nominating procedures. Brookings Institution, 104-105

[11] CQ Press. (1939). "Selection of nominees for the presidency."

[12] Ibid.

[13] Republican National Convention. (1893). Proceedings of the First Three Republican Conventions, 27.

[14] Ibid., 54.

[15] Ibid., 66.

[16] Proceedings of the 1860 Republican National Convention, 71.

[17] Ibid., 111.

[18] Ibid., 113.

[19] Ibid., 110.

[20] Official Proceedings of the Republican National Convention 1868, 75.

[21] Ibid., 76.

[22] Proceedings of the 1868 Republican National Convention, 94.

[23] New York Daily Tribune, May 28, 1880, p. 4.

[24] Becker, 76.

[25] Proceedings of the 1876 Republican National Convention, 34-35.

[26] Ibid., 88.

[27] Ibid.

[28] Ibid., 95-96.

[29] Ibid., 96.

[30] Ibid., 97.

[31] Ibid., 100.

[32] Becker, 77.

[33] New York Daily Tribune, May 28, 1880, p. 4

[34] Becker, 77.

[35] Ibid., 78.

[36] Ibid., 78-79.

[37] Ackerman, K.D. (2003). Dark Horse: The Surprise Election and Political Murder of President James A. Garfield, 23.

[38] Proceedings of the 1880 Republican National Convention, 43.

[39] Ibid., 156.

[40] Ibid., 31-32.

[41] Ibid., 32.

[42] Ibid., 198-271 (covering ballots #1-36).

[43] Ibid., 203-204.

[44] Ibid., 219.

[45] Proceedings of the 1884 Republican National Convention, 157.

[46] Proceedings of the 1892 Republican National Convention, 137.

[47] Proceedings of the 1912 Republican National Convention, 146-158.

[48] Ibid., 154.

[49] Ibid. See, for example, 180-184, 187-189, 195, 213-216, 366 (California's chair announced the delegation declined to vote, a Mr. Tryon challenged this and he and one other delegate had their votes in favor of the platform recorded while the other 24 delegates did not vote), 367-372, 391-401, and 404.

[50] "Pledge Illinois for Roosevelt, First and Last," Chicago Daily Tribune, April 20, 1912, p. 5.

[51] Proceedings of the 1912 Republican National Convention, 391-392.

[52] Ibid., 400.

[53] While Oregon's primary law clearly required the delegates to all vote for Roosevelt, Illinois' law is somewhat less certain – contemporary news accounts fail to mention delegates being legally bound, only referencing instructions from the party (see note xliii), and a published academic paper of the time says that the Illinois primary law only says the vote shall be

considered "advisory" (Aylsworth, L.E. (Aug. 1912). Presidential Primary Elections — Legislation of 1910-1912. The American Political Science Review, 6(3), 432-433). It is quite possible the Illinois delegation misunderstood or misspoke regarding the obligations supposedly imposed upon them by the state's new primary law.

[54] Proceedings of the 1920 Republican National Convention, 183-184.

[55] Ibid., 189.

[56] Ibid., 208.

[57] Ibid., 215-216.

[58] Ibid., 216-217.

[59] Ibid., 218.

[60] Ibid., 218.

[61] Ibid., 186-187.

[62] Ibid., 198.

[63] Ibid., 202-205.

[64] Ibid., 207-209.

[65] Ibid., 221. Maryland had cast all 16 of its ballots for Wood on the previous nine ballots, possibly due to the state's primary law binding delegates to vote for the winner of the state's primary "as long as in their conscientious judgment there is any possibility of his being nominated."

[66] Ibid., 230.

[67] Transcript of the Rules Committee of the 1964 Republican National Convention, 61.

[68] Ibid., 69.

[69] Ibid., 70.

[70] David, P.T., Goldman, R.M., & Bain, R.C. (1964). The Politics of National Party Conventions (Revised), Brookings Institution, 185.

Chapter 2 –
Ford, Reagan & the First Binding of GOP Delegates

After 120 years of rejecting the notion that delegates to the Republican convention could be bound, the 1976 rules changed course, but only after a lengthy fight in the rules committee.

The reason for the reversal was simple: incumbent President Gerald Ford faced a serious challenge from former California Gov. Ronald Reagan and was desperate to lock down as many delegates as possible. His campaign was concerned that many delegates who originally came to the convention pledged to him would defect and instead support his rival. In light of the longstanding tradition of respecting delegates' right to vote for whomever they supported, this was a very real concern. As one history of the 1976 campaign explained:

> Many state party rules did not bind delegates to vote for the candidate in whose name they were chosen, and while some states did have such rules, they were virtually unenforceable. It was rare for delegates to break with their candidate, but anything was possible in 1976. Besides, no one had ever gone to jail for voting for someone other than whom they were pledged at a national convention.[1]

Prior to the 1976 nomination contest, several states had passed laws requiring delegates elected through primaries to support the candidate to whom they originally pledged themselves. These laws were largely regarded as unconstitutional in light of a string of Supreme Court rulings including *Cousins v. Wigoda* and *Ripon Society Inc. v. Republican National Party*, all of them generally finding that the state did not have the authority to interfere in the internal affairs and decisions of a national political party, including such matters as credential decisions and how delegate votes are conducted (for further discussion, see Chapter 4).

Nonetheless, the Ford forces saw an opportunity, and they seized it through an amendment to Rule 18, which at that time contained the language written originally by James Garfield in 1880 in only slightly

modified form as well as the explicit ban on unit voting added in 1964. The proposed amendment would insert the following language into the rule after the Garfield language and before the 1964 language:

> [P]rovided, however, that in any event, the vote of each State for the nomination for President shall be announced and recorded (or in the absence of an announcement shall be recorded) in accordance with the results of any binding Presidential Primary or direct election of delegates bound or pledged pursuant to state law.

Explaining the amendment, Ford said the following in the days before the convention:

> [T]he Justice amendment, which we are proposing, would require that all delegates vote according to the laws under which they were selected. And I think that is a very proper amendment to carry out the wishes of the people that supported those individuals at the time they were chosen.[2]

As U.S. president, Ford was in control of the Republican Party machinery and it was fairly easy for his team to maneuver what became known as the "Justice Amendment" through earlier meetings of the Republican National Committee,[3] and now it was up to his forces to push it through the convention rules committee.

Legal counsel for the rules committee, identified as Mr. Cramer, listed several reasons why this rule change was needed,[4] although they are generally inconsistent or fail to acknowledge the longstanding principle and rule of the Republican Party that delegates arrive at the convention unbound.

His first reason was practical enough. Recognizing that several states had in recent years passed laws purporting to bind delegates to the results of primaries, he noted that delegates themselves often weren't elected by state parties in proportion to the primary results, and delegates might not know to which candidate they were supposedly bound and for whom they were supposed to vote if the delegation were polled.

Citing the Arkansas delegation, entitled to 27 total delegates and with 17 of them apparently pledged to Reagan, Cramer asked the following:

> Which are you? Which ten of those delegates, of the 27? Are you a four-delegate? And you are so designated. Are you the 17th? Any one of you are therefore Reagan delegates? That is not the way it was done in most of the states.
>
> Instead, they chose 27 delegates.
>
> Now, if you are going to have a poll of the delegation, how are you going to poll a delegation with a delegate not knowing which candidate to whom he is supposedly bound, and there is no way of determining it?[522]

This is a sensible enough concern, if one accepts that delegates can be bound. His second reason is sound as well – because many of the state laws binding delegates were of recent vintage, an addition to the rules was needed to clarify the situation.

Cramer then nullified his first two reasons upon offering his third reason for the rule's necessity:

> Because of the decision of *Cousins v. Wigoda* and the *Ripon* case, which clearly says that a party in its deliberations can do as it sees fit....
>
> Now, this raises the implication of any delegate who even though he is bound by state law under that decision could conceivably take the position that he did not have to be bound by state law under that court decision; that this was a political decision; he could make it as he sees fit.

In a later explanation of the need for the rule, Cramer went further than saying the two decisions (and others) "raise[] the implication" that a delegate might "conceivably take the position" they were free to vote their conscience, and described in fuller detail what the courts had held:

> [B]ecause this convention, under *Cousins v. Wigoda*, regardless of the state law, would have license to do what it saw fit according to its party rules....
>
> I am saying that *Cousins v. Wigoda* in effect said that the party can do as it sees fit with regard to delegate selection matters, even though it is totally contrary to state law. We in fact are saying in this amendment that because of *Cousins v. Wigoda* ... delegates could, without this resolution, vote contrary to State law.[6]

In other words, Cramer first argued the convention needed to adopt the Justice Amendment because recently passed state laws necessitated it, then explained that recent court decisions nullified those state laws. This is incoherent – if the laws were nullified (which they were), then there was no reason for the party to adopt rules conforming to them, at least not for anything other than political reasons.

> *"Cousins v. Wigoda in effect said that the party can do as it sees fit with regard to delegate selection matters, even though it is totally contrary to state law. We in fact are saying in this amendment that because of Cousins v. Wigoda ... delegates could, without this resolution, vote contrary to State law."*

The fourth reason Cramer provides is equally flawed. According to him, the chair of the convention, Republican House Minority Leader John Rhodes, had requested a rule that would give him guidance regarding the matter of supposedly bound delegates. He further states that Rhodes had conveyed to him his uncertainty over how he would have to rule if it came up on the convention floor:

> [B]asically, he says, "In the event your committee does not act, I may be forced to make a ruling from the Chair without any precedents or guidance from the Rules.

There are two problems with this statement. First, the fact that *Cousins v. Wigoda* had determined that a political party could "do as it sees fit," as Cramer aptly summarized the case, meant the whole issue was moot – there was no need for rules addressing state laws that had no force at the convention. More importantly, however, there was substantial precedent and guidance from the rules as well as past rulings of the chair, as documented in Chapter 1. In fact, since the original Garfield language was adopted into the Republican National Convention rules, more than 200 precedents existed to guide Rhodes' rulings.

As described in Chapter 1, the most definitive statement from the convention chair on this issue was at the 1876 convention, regarding the four delegates from Pennsylvania who asked on the second ballot that their votes be recorded for Blaine, not Hartranft, as the state convention had directed. The chair's initial ruling was that the four votes be recorded for Blaine, and he explained his decision with the following words:

> …[T]he chair rules that it is the right of any and every member equally, to vote his sentiments in the convention.[7]

After having his ruling upheld after extensive debate on the convention floor, the chair described the ruling this way:

> [I]t is the right of every individual member thereof to vote his individual sentiments.[8]

And as the Illinois and Oregon delegations demonstrated in 1912, state laws purporting to bind delegates were to be given exactly the same treatment as any other effort to deny a delegate the right to vote his or her conscience. As stipulated in the rule drafted by James Garfield in 1880, a poll of the delegation settled the matter every time, regardless of whether it was the custom of delegations, state party directions, or state law that attempted to bind delegates.

It's important to understand as well that the Justice Amendment was narrowly aimed at only 18 or 19 states that had fairly unambiguous laws purporting to bind delegates according to primary results. (Cramer used both numbers at different times.) According to a study by the Library of

Congress requested by Rhodes, 30 states had statutes regarding presidential preference primaries. In Cramer's remarks to the committee, he says the Library of Congress found 18 or 19 of those states' statutes were written in such a way that would bind delegates' votes according to the outcome of those primaries if the laws had been constitutional.

The fact that the Justice Amendment was limited to a minority of states indicates that it was still understood and unquestioned that delegates from states without such laws retained their full and traditional right to cast their votes according to their conscience, even in states that had held primaries but did not explicitly attempt to bind delegates through state law.

One rules committee member, identified as Mr. Milligan of Indiana, noted the freedom that delegates had previously enjoyed in voting their consciences. Speaking in favor of the Justice Amendment, he noted that the effect of state laws binding delegates according to primary results meant that "[w]e no longer have delegates coming to a national convention willy-nilly to do as they so desire."[9]

Implicit in that statement is that even if state laws on delegates were applicable, they would not apply to delegates from states without such laws. As Mr. Milligan might put it, every other delegate remained free to vote "willy-nilly … as they so desire."

Opponents of the Justice Amendment focused primarily on the fact that it would put the convention in the position of determining which state laws were in force, how they applied, and how to enforce them.

After noting that the language of the amendment was "fraught with legal complexities," Dick Derham of Washington disputed that they could or should enforce any binding of delegates, noting that the laws on the matter were not in effect:

> Here is the most recent declaration for interpretation of the law
> from an official in the State of Oregon. He was asked.... What is
> the legal binding upon delegates at their National Party Convention
> of the statutory provisions?
>
> He states, "However, it is clear that the National Convention is not
> under any legal obligation to either accept the delegates selected

under the Oregon statute nor is it required to honor the pledge required by that statute."[10]

According to Derham, he had a similar statement from Texas declaring that state's binding law unenforceable.

Following extensive debate and discussion, both for and against, the Justice Amendment was adopted by the rules committee on a voice vote – Ford allies dominated the rules committee, and it was easy for them to push it through.[11]

> "It is clear that the National Convention is not under any legal obligation to either accept the delegates selected under the Oregon statute nor is it required to honor the pledge required by that statute."

A substantial debate might have been expected on the floor of the convention, which would have to vote to accept or reject the changed rule that would allow the binding of delegate votes for the first time in Republican National Convention history. But the Reagan forces instead put their efforts into passing an amendment to Rule 16, which would have required both Ford and Reagan to name their vice-presidential nominees before voting on the presidential nominee began (Reagan had announced his choice prior to the convention, while Ford had not).

Reagan's campaign manager, John Sears, had concocted the Rule 16 amendment for two purposes. It was first intended as a test of strength, in order to demonstrate that support for the former California governor went beyond those delegates that were publicly pledged to him. The second goal was to force Ford into a decision that might cost him support among delegates, flipping them over to Reagan.[12]

But following fierce lobbying and pressure by the Ford team, Sears' gambit came up short – 1,069 delegates voted for the amendment to Rule 16, with 1,180 voting against.[13] With only 1,130 votes needed to win the nomination, it appeared that the convention was firmly in the hands of the Ford forces. Following that dispiriting loss on Rule 16, the Reagan team did not contest the Rule 18 change, and the remainder of the rules committee report was adopted by a voice vote.[14] The roll call the next evening for

the presidential nomination had a nearly identical tally – 1,187 for Ford and 1,070 for Reagan.

It wasn't only the new language in Rule 18 that denied some delegates their long-held right to vote according to their own consciences. In Mississippi, the state party had long used the unit rule, allowing the majority to dictate how the state's entire vote would be cast. The delegation had arrived nearly evenly split between Ford and Reagan, but after extensive deliberations among the delegation over whether to use the unit rule, it was decided to continue the past practice. Ford narrowly won the delegation's internal vote, meaning that all 30 of the state's votes went against the Reagan team's amendment to Rule 16.[15]

The use of the unit rule to determine Mississippi's vote on the Rule 16 amendment raises the question of why it was allowed. The simple answer is that it was permitted because no delegate objected to it on the floor of the convention: The language of the Republican Party's longstanding rule on the matter gives every delegate the right to challenge the announcement of the vote by the delegation chair – but if no delegate objects, then the use of the unit rule or any other effort to deny delegates the right to cast their votes freely cannot be detected and corrected.

A single delegate from Mississippi could have, during the roll call on the Rule 16 amendment, objected to the announcement of 30 votes against, and the chair would have been required to conduct a poll of the delegates. So why didn't that happen?

The book *Reagan's Revolution: The Untold Story of the Campaign That Started It All* provides an extensive explanation what happened with the Mississippi delegation in 1976.[16] The short version is, the delegation had customarily used the unit rule in order to maximize their leverage at the convention, and it was decided by a vote of all the delegates and alternates to maintain it. Nevertheless, at least one Ford backer in the delegation said he would demand a poll of the delegation if all 30 of Mississippi's votes were announced for Reagan under the unit rule.[17]

Although the Mississippi delegation voted under the unit rule on the Rule 16 amendment, they later met and voted to abandon it before the roll call for the presidential nomination – Mississippi's votes were split, with 16 given to Ford and 14 to Reagan[18] (Mississippi was not among the 18 or 19 states bound under the Justice Amendment).

While the 1976 convention allowed delegates from certain states to be bound, the proceedings show the rule was unpopular with many. Two delegations in fact used the roll call vote for the presidential nomination to voice their displeasure, the first one offering a modest rebuke, the other far harsher.

At least one Ford backer in the delegation said he would demand a poll of the delegation if all 30 of Mississippi's votes were announced for Reagan under the unit rule.

When North Carolina was called, the delegation chair first voiced displeasure that the microphone had been turned off the previous day when he was attempting to get a roll call vote, an act he called "tyranny." Then he made the following statement regarding the state's 54 votes:

> North Carolina, the state that gave Ronald Reagan his first primary victory, and with 51 delegates on the floor favoring his nomination, is required by State law on the first ballot to cast 29 votes for Ronald Reagan, 25 votes for Gerald Ford.[19]

The South Dakota delegation went further than the North Carolina delegation – it simply refused to announce its votes, forcing the chair to do so. The proceedings record the following exchange:

> GEORGEANNE SORENSON of South Dakota – South Dakota, a land of grass roots believes in the preservation of the land of opportunity and joins the majority of Americans who voted in favor of Ronald Reagan. Madam Secretary, South Dakota yields to the Chair to cast South Dakota's vote, in accordance to Rule 18.

> CHIEF READING CLERK – In accordance with Rule 18, the Chairman has directed that for South Dakota, 11 votes be cast for Reagan, 9 votes for Ford.[20]

Although the conscience protections of Rule 18 weren't available on the presidential nomination roll call to delegates from the 19 states bound

under the Justice Amendment, they were available to those from the remaining states and territories. Herbert Morgan, a delegate from Virginia, invoked the conscience protections after Virginia's votes were announced as 35 votes for Reagan and 16 votes for Ford, and the convention chair promptly directed the secretary to poll the delegation.[21]

The results were identical following the delegation poll, but two important points were reinforced by Morgan's action – first, that upon the requesting of any delegate the chair is duty-bound to order the secretary to poll the delegation, and second, that the protections are not simply to guard against the old unit rule. If, in fact, the Garfield language were only written and enforced with the unit rule in mind, then the chair would not have ordered a poll of the delegation, since the results had been announced as split between the two candidates.

It is also worth noting that the 1976 convention featured two other invocations of conscience protections on other roll calls. During the vote on the vice-presidential nominee, an Alabama delegate requested the delegation be polled, and the chair immediately ordered it done (although it was probably out of order at the time, since the Alabama results had not yet been announced).[22] In addition, a delegate from New Jersey requested a roll call on the Reagan campaign's proposed amendment to Rule 16, and again the request was immediately honored (and like the Alabama results, the initially announced results were split, four yes, 62 no, and one abstention, and the delegation poll likewise upheld the original announced results).[23]

At the 1980 Republican convention, Reagan's forces were clearly in control, and the discussion in the rules committee reflected their intent to undo the changes made at the previous convention. The committee's staff had not even bothered to put together a list of which states had state laws purporting to bind delegates – one sign of how little expectation there was that the 1980 convention would continue to recognize delegate binding.[24]

Explaining an amendment that would delete the 1976 language binding delegates to the results of state primaries, Roger Yurchuck of Ohio offered the following explanation:

> This amendment merely gets this committee and the Convention
> back on the road it was on prior to 1978 [sic]. This amendment was

put in in 1976 as a result of some political shenanigans at that time. Now we are just going back to the old way.[25]

A number of practical issues were offered in support of eliminating the 1976 language, with a Mr. Beard of North Carolina offering a little levity in his remarks:

> Another question I must ask, because I have looked into it myself, according to my interpretation of North Carolina's primary law, if we do not delete 18(a) language, we must cast 30 votes for the former Governor of California and 10 votes for an elusive gentleman by the name of "No preference." I believe the people of Illinois, of Massachusetts, of Connecticut, and of possibly New Hampshire, will find themselves in the envious position at this Convention of casting their votes for a left-wing lunatic by the name of John Anderson. I would not impose that burden upon the conscience of any Republican.[26]

Another committee member, Connecticut national committeeman John Alsop, spoke in favor of removing the 1976 language. After first noting that state laws binding delegates according to primary results were likely unconstitutional and therefore could be safely ignored, he offered the following statement:

> I believe we should go back to our previous wording. I think that the delegates who have been seated by this convention should vote their convictions in the full knowledge of the laws

"If we do not delete 18(a) language... I believe the people of Illinois, of Massachusetts, of Connecticut, and of possibly New Hampshire, will find themselves in the envious position at this Convention of casting their votes for a left-wing lunatic by the name of John Anderson. I would not impose that burden upon the conscience of any Republican."

which apply to them and go back home if they vacate them and take their medicine.

When the vote was called (technically, two votes – one to accept the amendment stripping out the 1976 language, and another to pass the newly amended Rule 18), there was not a single "no" vote recorded on either question.

And with that, the Republican Party's lone foray into binding delegates to prevent them from voting their convictions was over.

---

[1] Shirley, C. (2005). Reagan's Revolution: The Untold Story of the Campaign That Started It All. 200-201.

[2] The Presidency Project at the University of California-Santa Barbara. (1976). Transcript of President Ford news conference, July 19, 1976. Available online at: http://www.presidency.ucsb.edu/ws/?pid=6215.

[3] Shirley, 61, 252.

[4] Transcript of the rules committee of the Republican National Convention. (1976). 208-211.

[5] Ibid., 209.

[6] Ibid., 265.

[7] Proceedings of the 1876 Republican National Convention, 88.

[8] Ibid., 100.

[9] Transcript of the rules committee of the 1976 Republican National Convention, 252.

[10] Ibid., 216.

[11] CQ Almanac. (1976). 1976 Republican Convention Divided Republicans Nominate Ford and Dole, 32, 892-99.

[12] Apple, R.W. (August 18, 1976.) Ford Gains and Blocks Reagan on Disclosure of a No. 2 Choice; Baker or Ruckelshaus Favored. The New York Times.

[13] Ibid.

[14] CQ Almanac, 892-99.

[15] Ibid.

[16] See Shirley, Chapter 13: "Bloody Mississippi," 283-296, for the full history of the Mississippi delegation's travails at the 1976 Republican National Convention.

[17] Ibid, 289 – 290.

[18] Ibid.

[19] Proceedings of the 1976 Republican National Convention, 416.

[20] Ibid., 418.

[21] Ibid., 418-419.

[22] Ibid., 444.

[23] Ibid., 254.

[24] Transcript of the rules committee of the Republican National Convention. (1980). 64.

[25] Ibid., p. 57.

[26] Ibid., p. 63.

Chapter 3 –
Muddying the Waters in the Rules Committee

From 1980 until the present, the Republican Party has maintained the pre-1976 language protecting delegates against efforts to bind their votes at the convention. The most notable official change was that in 1984, the 1964 language on unit voting became a stand-alone rule instead of being incorporated into the same rule as the language originally written by James Garfield. In 2012, the explicit prohibition on unit voting was Rule 38 while the Garfield language was included in Rule 37. In addition, language directing the convention chair to report the results of the poll at the end of the balloting of the states was added in 2012.

One of the subtler changes to the rules during this period was not technically a change – it was simply a re-ordering of the rules. Prior to 2000, the rules governing the convention appeared at the beginning of the rules report, while the rules establishing and governing the Republican National Committee (RNC) from the end of the convention until the beginning of the next, appeared at the end. In between these two sections were rules governing the convening of the next convention, describing among other things how many delegates each state would be able to send to the convention and the time periods in which states could hold primaries, caucuses, or conventions.[1] Instead, in 2000 and without any discussion, the order was flipped, with the section containing the RNC rules coming first and the convention rules coming last, with the rules regarding convening the next convention maintaining their position in the middle.

This is how what was Rule 13 in 1996 became Rule 38 in 2000 – the Republican convention did not adopt a large number of new rules, it simply pushed the convention rules to the end.

Unfortunately, this flipping of the order may create the impression that the two sets of rules appearing before the convention rules are in effect or applicable to that year's national convention. But the order reversal did not alter the effect or application of any rule or the time frame in which the different sets of rules were in effect.

The preamble to the 2012 rules adopted at that year's national convention spell out clearly the duration of those rules:

> BE IT FURTHER RESOLVED, That the following be and hereby
> are adopted as *The Rules of the Republican Party*, composed of the
> rules for the election and government of the Republican National
> Committee until the next national convention, the rules under
> which delegates and alternate delegates shall be allotted to the
> respective states in the next national convention, and the rules
> under which such delegates and alternate delegates shall be elected
> and under which contests shall be considered, and the rules of
> business of this national convention.

Upon a careful reading, it's clear that the first two sections concerning the Republican National Committee take effect beginning at the conclusion of the convention at which the rules were adopted, while the section on convention rules is in force at the convention where it is adopted, not the next one.

The final rule adopted at the 2012 convention, Rule 42, more explicitly explains the dates in which the newly passed convention rules are in effect:

> Upon adoption of the report of the Convention Committee on Rules
> and Order of Business, Rule Nos. 26–42 shall constitute the
> Standing Rules for this convention and the temporary rules for the
> next convention.

The switching of the order may leave the impression that the convention is the conclusion of the four-year establishment of the RNC, as opposed to being the beginning. But the preamble and final rule make clear – at the beginning of every convention, new rules are adopted to re-establish the RNC, and they govern its operations from the conclusion of the convention until the beginning of the next.

Rule 42 also makes clear that, in the time between the convening of the convention and the adoption of a new set of rules, the old rules are in effect – this is why they are called temporary rules. This means that until the 2016 convention passes new rules, the rules governing the 2012 convention are in effect.

This interpretation is not controversial – respected Republican lawyer Benjamin Ginsberg, who has served as general counsel to the Republican National Committee and four presidential campaigns, affirmed the status of the temporary rules in a March 2016 interview on the MSNBC network. Discussing Rule 40, which in 2012 required among other things that a candidate must have majority support in at least eight delegations in order to be officially nominated, Ginsberg said the following:

> **At the beginning of every convention, new rules are adopted to re-establish the RNC, and they govern its operations from the conclusion of the convention until the beginning of the next.**

> In fact, that's not a rule. That's part of what's called the temporary rules. Each convention has to pass for itself the number of states that put a candidate's name in nomination.... The 2016 convention and its rules committee has to make that decision. So there is no eight-state rule in effect right now for the next convention.... The 2016 convention can make that number one, eight, 18, 28 or 58, if it wishes.[2]

The potential confusion and inconsistency inspired by the reordering of the rules in 2000 is relatively modest in comparison to later developments in the rules, however. Although these later developments did not change the rules governing the convention and delegate voting as the Justice Amendment of 1976 did, they did change the rules governing the call to convention in ways that either directly or indirectly challenge the delegate conscience protections.

Prior to 2008, the rules in the middle section governing the convening of the next convention included language in several places referencing either the "election" or "selection" of delegates. For example, the 2004 version included the following in Rule 14(b):

> Participation in a Republican primary, caucus, or any meeting or convention held for the purpose of selecting delegates and alternate delegates to a county, district, state, or national convention shall in

no way be abridged for reasons of sex, race, religion, color, age, or national origin...

Likewise, Rule 15(a) included the following language in 2004:

Delegates at large and their alternate delegates and delegates from congressional districts and their alternate delegates to the national convention shall be elected in the following manner...

In 2008, however, the rules that were adopted included language that added either "elect" or "select" in most places where one or the other terms appeared, and most importantly also inserted "allocate" and "bind" (or their derivations, such as "allocating" and "bound") throughout the rules for calling the next convention as well. So Rule 14(b) was changed to read:

Participation in a Republican primary, caucus, or any meeting or convention held for the purpose of electing, selecting, *allocating*, or *binding* delegates and alternate delegates to a county, district, state, or national convention shall in no way be abridged for reasons of sex, race, religion, color, age, or national origin.... [emphasis added]

And 15(a) read as follows in the rules adopted for 2008:

Delegates at large and their alternate delegates and delegates from congressional districts and their alternate delegates to the national convention shall be elected, selected, *allocated*, or *bound* in the following manner... [emphasis added]

Given that Republican convention rules for more than 150 years had consistently rejected the idea that delegates could be bound (except for the 1976 convention) and affirmed repeatedly that all delegates were free to vote their consciences on any and all matters brought to a vote, the adoption of this language was wildly inconsistent with past practice,

particularly since the Garfield language that protects against binding also remained in 2008.

The change was initially offered at a meeting of the Republican National Committee's rules committee, which is separate from the convention's rules committee. Gathering just two days before the convention rules committee would meet, attendees were discussing changes that would be offered when the convention rules committee met.

The addition of the terms "allocate" and "bind" were not offered as substantive changes, and in fact the initial proposal did not include the term "bind" at all. Explaining the proposed changes to past rules, RNC legal staffer Jennifer Shaheen described the amendments including the addition of "allocate" as "just a package of technical amendments."[3]

After going through several other technical changes, Sheehan described the purpose of the amendment:

> The last amendment, it applies to throughout the rules the definition of "elect," "select" and/or "allocate." It just allows the clarification that applies across the board during the delegate selection process.[4]

The rules committee member from Utah, Nancy Lord, then asked if "allocate" was in reference to "the binding of delegates."[5] After Sheehan replied in the affirmative, Lord requested the term "bind" be added as well, so the amendment would now insert both "allocate" and "bind" as well as either "elect" or "select" throughout the section. This was the full extent of the discussion of what was presented as a technical amendment but that suggested a change in a principle of the Republican National Convention dating back to the party's first convention in 1856.

It's important to note the differences between allocation and binding in this context. Allocation refers to the number of delegates a candidate is nominally awarded as a result of a primary or other contest, such as a caucus. For example, Florida allocates all of its delegates on what is known as a "winner-take-all" basis, meaning that the candidate receiving the most votes in the primary will theoretically see every delegate slot filled with a delegate committed to support them. Other states allocate

delegates according to other formulas, or don't hold presidential preference contests at all.

But in order to fill their allocated delegate slots with supporters, campaigns must identify those supporters and get them elected or selected to those slots.

Binding, on the other hand, refers to attempting to impose a predetermined vote on a particular delegate, regardless of whether that delegate wishes to vote that way. In cases where delegate slots are filled with supporters of the candidate they are allocated to, binding is generally unnecessary – these are typically among a candidate's most devoted supporters, and there is little need to impose a requirement on them to vote for the candidate they are already committed to.

So the key distinction between the two terms is that allocation addresses how many delegates a candidate can expect to be supporters from a particular delegation, while binding is aimed at requiring delegates to vote for the candidate they have been allocated to. While there is some obvious interplay between the terms, they are very different.

Earlier in the day, before Sheehan offered her opinion that allocation was in reference to the binding of delegates, there had already been a discussion of binding related to the party's rules imposing sanctions on state delegations if their state had held a primary before the allowed date. And that discussion seems to acknowledge that it was and remained the longstanding practice of the national convention to ignore the binding of delegates.

Bill Crocker, the national committeeman from Texas who would become the RNC's general counsel in 2011, offered the following amendment to Rule 15(b)(2):

> The Republican Party of any State or territory by rule duly adopted
> may prohibit any delegate to the national convention from that
> State or territory from being bound or required to vote for a certain
> nominee by or in accordance with the results of any presidential
> primary, caucus, convention, or other election or meeting held in
> that State or territory.[6]

In discussing his amendment, Crocker noted the following:

It is my understanding that the language I propose is the present interpretation of the national party rules, but it is not expressed explicitly in the national party rules. This is not going to allow any delegate to do anything independently of the direction of his or her State party. This is simply an attempt to express what is my understanding is the current national rules by implication and interpretation.[7]

Discussion against the amendment did not challenge Crocker's assertion that this reflected the current understanding of the convention's rules on binding; instead it was focused on how it might affect penalties imposed on states that held primaries prior to the allowed time frame.

The meeting of the convention rules committee two days later contains no direct discussion of the addition of the terms "allocate" and "bind" to the rules. A staffer from the RNC general counsel's office, Tom Josefiak, also asserted that of the amendments proposed and adopted in the previous week, which would have included the meeting two days earlier, the only substantive amendments concerned who could be officers of the RNC, how minutes of committee meetings should be distributed, and that only New Hampshire and South Carolina could hold primaries before March 1.[8] The Crocker amendment was adopted by the convention rules committee, although it did not make it into the final rules adopted at the convention.

> **If McCain were elected, as an incumbent president he would be able to use the binding of delegates to help ward off any challenge to his re-nomination.**

It's difficult to understand how the term "bind" came to be included in the Republican rules in such a casual manner, with almost no discussion or debate and with it being characterized as a "technical" amendment instead of a substantive one.

One possibility is that the campaign of Arizona Sen. John McCain, who as the presumptive nominee held immense sway over the rules committee, was attempting to sneak something into the rules that it thought might be politically advantageous to him in 2012. If McCain were elected, as an incumbent president he would be able to use the binding of

delegates to help ward off any challenge to his re-nomination, similar to how binding of delegates was used to thwart Ronald Reagan's challenge to President Gerald Ford in 1976.[9]

Another possibility is that the legal counsel's staff simply didn't understand the importance of what they were doing in adding the term "bind" to the rules. The fact that it wasn't even included in the original package of technical amendments but was instead an amendment to an amendment offered from the floor with minimal discussion at the close of the RNC rules committee meeting (this was the final amendment voted on in the meeting), easily lends itself to the interpretation that what appears to have been a monumental change to a long-held principle was simply done in error and without understanding.

That said, there is another possibility, that the counsel's office was drawing a fine distinction between whether a state was permitted to pass resolutions, require pledges, or otherwise attempt to bind delegates to support specific candidates, and the longstanding rules and rulings from the chair refusing to enforce such binding and calling for a poll of delegates any time a delegate requested to have his or her true vote recorded.

Another possibility is that the counsel's office in 2008 was attempting to anticipate the process for the next convention, in 2012. The rules under consideration at the 2008 meeting where the language regarding binding was added would not have had any effect at all upon the 2008 delegate election and selection process, which was already completed, but were for the 2012 nomination process. If the legal counsel's office anticipated that by the 2012 convention the Rule 37 protections for delegates to vote their conscience would be altered, weakened, or removed, then the inclusion of references to binding in the rules approved in 2008 may have been appropriate.

Regardless of why or how the references to binding of delegates was added to the rules in 2008, the fact remains that the protections for delegates to the national convention remained in the rules for 2012. On the surface this may seem to have created a conflict, with the section of the rules covering the convening of the 2012 convention containing language recognizing binding while Rule 37 and Rule 38, contained in the convention rules section, effectively prohibit such binding.

But there is no conflict, for the simple reason that the rules governing the convening of the convention expire at the start of that convention and have no authority as to how the convention is run. Instead, each convention establishes its own rules, and in 2012 the standing rules approved by the Republican National Convention retained the full, historical protections for delegates contained in Rule 37 and Rule 38.

> **Rules governing the convening of the convention expire at the start of that convention and have no authority as to how the convention is run. Instead, each convention establishes its own rules.**

The rules approved at the 2012 convention included similar language (still in the section governing the convening of the next [2016] convention) regarding the binding of delegates, but those rules also expire at the start of the next convention, and without a change to the standing rules of the convention they cannot be used to bind delegates to vote against their consciences. So while at first glance the rules appear to endorse binding, the language suggesting this is the case is not in effect at the 2016 convention unless there are changes to the standing rules of the convention.

This is true as well of an amendment to the rules adopted in April 2013 governing the convening of the 2016 convention. This change represented the most direct challenge to the Republican convention's conscience protections since the Ford campaign amended the rules in 1976.

At the April 10 meeting in Los Angeles of the Republican National Committee's rules committee, the following language was added to Rule 16 as a new section (a):

> 1) Any statewide presidential preference vote that permits a choice among candidates for the Republican nomination for President of the United States in a primary, caucus, or a state convention must be used to allocate and bind the state's delegation to the national convention in either a proportional or winner-take-all manner, except for delegates and alternate delegates who appear on a ballot in a statewide election and are elected directly by primary voters.

2) The Secretary of the Convention shall faithfully announce and record each delegate's vote in accordance with the delegate's obligation under these rules, state law, or state party rule. If any delegate bound by these rules, state party rules or state law to vote for a presidential candidate at the national convention demonstrates support under Rule 40 for any person other than the candidate to whom he or she is bound, such support shall not be recognized. Except as provided for by state law or state party rule, no presidential candidate shall have the power to remove a delegate.

What prompted such a radical departure from the principle that every delegate at the Republican National Convention was free to vote his or her conscience in all matters? The simplest answer is the rules committee was trying to undo what it considered to be the damage caused at the 2012 convention by supporters of Rep. Ron Paul of Texas.

During the nomination process, Paul's campaign finished in third or fourth place in most of the early contests, although he did finish second in New Hampshire and a few other states. Rick Santorum became the primary rival to former Massachusetts Gov. Mitt Romney, with Paul rarely seen as a serious challenger for the nomination.

But Paul's campaign organized extensively in several states in order to earn delegates to the national convention, and many of his supporters managed to get elected at state conventions. In many states, party rules ostensibly bound them to vote for Romney, but they ignored those instructions and voted for Paul instead.

The end result of this maneuvering was that delegates ostensibly bound to Romney voted for Paul, and while they were not recorded because Paul had not been officially placed in nomination, they also were not moved or recorded instead for Romney.

For example, in the Nevada caucuses Paul had finished in third place while Romney had won by nearly 30 points. Under the rules of the state party, Romney was allocated 14 of 28 delegates, while Paul was allocated five (former Speaker of the House Newt Gingrich was allocated six, and Santorum three). But during the roll call of the states the vote was announced as five for Romney, 17 for Paul, and five abstentions. The secretary repeated the announced vote simply as "Nevada, 5, Romney."[10]

It wasn't only Paul votes that were accorded this treatment – votes cast for Rep. Michelle Bachman, former Colorado Gov. Buddy Roemer, and Santorum were also not recorded. But there was no effort by the convention chair or secretary to force delegates to vote other than as their conscience dictated, or to record their votes for another candidate. Even with the language concerning the binding delegates in the call to convention, the conscience protections of Rule 37 remained in force.

At that 2012 convention, the Romney campaign also tried to give the presumptive nominee's campaign the power to deny credentials to delegates that in its view were supposed to be pledged to Romney but had indicated they might vote for another candidate, primarily Paul. This proved wildly unpopular with the delegates.

As a result, the RNC rules committee in April 2013 attempted to deal with what it thought of as the problem of "rogue" delegates who voted contrary to the instructions given them by state law, party rule, or other binding efforts.

Prior to the 2012 convention, such a rule change could not have occurred because rule changes were only permitted at the convention itself. In 2012, however, the convention approved Rule 12, which gave the Republican National Committee the power to change rules between conventions if a 75 percent supermajority approved. Following the RNC rules committee meeting, the full Republican National Committee approved the addition to Rule 16.

However, this new language – seeking to bind delegates and stripping them of the freedom to vote their conscience – suffers from the same fatal defect as the 2008 changes, when "allocate" and "bind" were added throughout the section on the convening of the next convention. The language will expire upon the start of the 2016 convention and will not be part of the standing rules of that convention.

> **The new language, which seeks to bind delegates and strip them of the freedom to vote their conscience, will expire upon the start of the 2016 convention and will not be part of the standing rules of that convention.**

The two separate components of the new Rule 16(a) language have different implications. Because (a)(1) addresses how delegates are to be elected and selected, it is clearly in the correct section of the rules, which specifically govern that subject. But it also clearly conflicts with the Rule 37 protections for delegates' freedom to vote their consciences. This may be a moot point by the time the convention opens, however, since the delegates will have already been elected according to the new language.

Rule 16(a)(2) on the other hand will clearly have no relevance at the 2016 Republican National Convention, having expired along with every other rule not included in the temporary rules of the convention. Even if identical language is approved in the same position at the convention, it will still only be in effect from the end of the 2016 convention until the start of the 2020 convention, where it will then expire again without effect.

To be in effect in 2016, the procedure outlined in 16(b) must be adopted as part of the standing rules of the convention, presumably in Rule 37 which governs roll call votes, similar to how the Ford campaign added binding language in 1976 as part of its effort to deny Reagan the nomination.

The fact that the language contained in Rule 16(b) does not apply to the proceedings of the convention would seem to be confirmed by a ruling of the convention rules committee chair in 2012. Addressing the issue of binding delegates, the committee was considering an amendment that would have included the following language in Rule 15:

> For any manner of binding or allocating delegates permitted by these rules, no delegate or alternate delegate who is bound or allocated to a particular presidential candidate may be certified under Rule 19 if the presidential candidate to whom the delegate or alternate delegate is bound or allocated has, in consultation with the state party, disavowed the delegate or alternate delegate.[11]

When a point of order was raised that this amendment would conflict with the no-binding provisions of Rule 37 and Rule 38, the committee chair, former New Hampshire Gov. John Sununu, rejected the point with the following ruling:

> The reason for denying it is that the rules you refer to, 37 and 38,
> apply to the casting of votes, and the section we are discussing here
> is the selection of delegates. That's why it's inconsistent.

Sununu's ruling summarizes the situation plainly – the section on delegate selection is separate and distinct from the section on voting, and the lack of a conflict presumably stems from the fact that the section on delegate selection expires before any voting takes place.

So why was the 16(a) language purporting to bind delegates and the earlier 2008 language adding "binding" language to the rules inserted into a section that would not be in force at the convention when roll call votes are taken? One possibility is that the confusion caused by the re-ordering of the rules in 2000, discussed above, led some to believe that it would be in effect for a time period that, at least in the way the rules now read, came after the selection of delegates.

A likelier reason, at least regarding the 16(a) language, is that it was the only place it could be added at the time. Rule 12, added in 2013 by the Republican National Convention, prohibited any amendment to the temporary convention rules (which are also the standing rules of the past convention). The relevant part of Rule 12 reads:

> The Republican National Committee may, by three-fourths (3/4)
> vote of its entire membership, amend Rule Nos. 1–11 and 13–25.

Simply put, the binding language was inserted where it was, in a section that would expire before the convention, because there was no mechanism for an amendment to the section where it needed to go to take effect, in either the temporary or permanent rules.

Although the additions to the rules in 2008, 2012, and 2013 won't be in effect unless added to the permanent rules for the 2016 convention, it is clear that the past two conventions have seen a serious decline in both the understanding of and appreciation for one of the longstanding principles of the Republican National Convention: that delegates are free to vote their consciences on all matters before them, including the presidential nomination. Chapter 5 of this book will examine in greater detail the importance of the conscience protections and why they are worth maintaining.

[1] Prior to 1956 the rules for convening the next convention appeared immediately before the convention rules, but the rules establishing and governing the Republican National Committee have always appeared after the convention rules.

[2] McCaskill, N.D. (March 9, 2016). GOP superlawyer on contested convention rule: 'In fact, that's not a rule.' Politico.

[3] Meeting of the Committee on Rules, 2008 Republican National Committee. (August 17, 2008). 93.

[4] Ibid., 105.

[5] Ibid.

[6] Ibid., 23-24.

[7] Ibid., p. 26.

[8] Transcript of the 2008 Republican National Convention Rules Committee Meeting. (August 29, 2008). 12-13.

[9] For discussion of how much power presumptive nominees can have at the national convention, see the transcript of the meeting of the Republican national convention committee on rules and order of business for the 2012 convention, in particular the comments of Henry Barbour of Mississippi beginning on page 91 and John Ryder of Tennessee beginning on page 95.

[10] Proceedings of the 2012 Republican National Convention, 394.

[11] Transcript of the 2012 Republican National Convention rules committee meeting. (August 24, 2012). 250.

Chapter 4 –
Delegates vs. Party Rules and State Law

While the national party has, with the single exception of 1976, never recognized or enforced at a national convention any effort to bind delegates according to state party instructions or state law, there have been numerous efforts both successful and unsuccessful to impose such requirements at the state level.

As Chapter 1 recounts, Maryland's delegation in 1860 was given a "recommendation" from the state party to support Rep. Edward Bates of Missouri for president; the 1868 convention roll call includes numerous references to "instructions" from the home state to vote for Ulysses S. Grant; and the 1876 and 1880 conventions included several delegations with instructions to vote as a unit for certain candidates as well. And the Michigan delegation in 1920 appears to have attempted to impose the unit rule in support of Hiram Johnson, only to be undone by the conscience protections embedded in the James Garfield language.

In addition, at the 1976 convention the Mississippi delegation voted according to the unit rule on the question of whether to force President Gerald Ford to name his running mate ahead of the roll call for the nomination, although it did not vote according to the unit rule on the presidential nomination itself.

State laws purporting to bind delegates have likewise been a common feature following legislation adopted in the years after the 1968 conventions, largely driven by Democrats. By 1976, at least 18 states had laws on the books directing convention delegates to vote according to the results of primaries.

And prior to this time, several states had passed primary election laws during the "Progressive Era" that also attempted to force delegates to vote according to primary results, beginning with Oregon in 1910. A *Corvallis Gazette-Times* article from April 1912 noted that Oregon's 10 delegates were obligated to vote for Theodore Roosevelt at the GOP convention "no matter their personal preference."[1] As noted in Chapter 1, Oregon's delegation ignored these instructions and relied on the Garfield language to ensure delegates had the right to do so.

The previous chapters discussed the history of the Republican National Convention's general defiance of instructions from state parties and state legislatures that seek to bind delegates to vote for or against certain candidates. This chapter will address why such binding instructions are null and void at the national convention, first addressing state party efforts and second addressing laws passed by state legislatures.

The first issue, regarding state party instructions, is relatively easy to understand – state party rules cannot conflict with national convention rules, and in the event that they do, the national convention rules will be supreme over the state party rules. This has been observed and noted on many occasions, including the following description in the book *The American Political Party System*:

> Republicans tend to leave it to the states to select national convention delegates, but they understand that their national party law will take precedence in any dispute.[2]

The supremacy of national rules over state rules has been well established in past Republican National Conventions. While this may seem at odds with the party's general preference today for greater local control and less centralized authority in terms of public policy, this position may in part stem from the Republican Party's original stance as more sympathetic to national power over state and local control. An academic paper on the unit rule published in 1899 described the Republicans' then-dominant thinking in this way:

> The Republican party… had its origin in discussions over a question of moral right and justice. Its formative period was at a time, not when powers were to be estimated, but when rights were to be asserted; its existence did not depend on interpretation, but on force. It looked eagerly to the central government for the exercise of this force as the only power through which its own principles could be maintained. It turned to the central government, not because of its theories, but because of its necessities…. [I]t is not strange that the tendency of such a party should make for centralism and not for localism.[3]

The argument that a state party should have the authority regardless of national party rules to bind its delegates to vote against their wishes was put forth at the 1880 convention, not only in discussion of the conscience protections offered by the Garfield language but also in a credentials challenge to several Alabama and Illinois delegates that was decided on the floor of the convention.[4]

At the Alabama state convention, James T. Rapier was elected as a delegate from the state's fourth congressional district, with the provision that he (and every other delegate) pledge to support the nomination of Ulysses S. Grant for president. Rapier refused to do so, and the Alabama state party then denied him his credentials and instead attempted to seat another delegate in his place. Two other delegates from the seventh congressional district, William H. Smith and Willard Warner, were denied credentials for similar reasons (there was also a dispute related to the voting process for these two delegates), and two replacement delegates willing to pledge their support to Grant were instead given credentials by the state party.[5]

The report of the credentials committee briefly summarized the facts of the dispute, and recommended in its report that Rapier, Smith and Warner be seated as delegates, not the substitutes willing to pledge their support to Grant. In the minority report of the credentials committee, supporting the seating of the substitute delegates, the following argument was made:

> [T]he majority propose for the adoption of this convention an *ex post facto* rule which will operate with great injustice, and virtually asserts the power of this National Convention of seating delegates chosen in violation of the long-established usages of the Republican party of the States to be affected thereby.[6]

The minority report also included the following regarding a series of credential challenges in the Illinois delegation that concerned the asserted power of state parties to bind delegates:

> [T]he majority of the Republicans of the State of Illinois, assembled in State conventions, pursuant to the call, proceeding from the

legitimate, official source, declared their preference for Ulysses S. Grant, and instructed the delegates to the convention to vote as a unit for him. Is this Convention to say that the majority of the convention of the State of Illinois possessed no such power?

Will this convention undertake to say, and with the country justify it in saying that the majority of the people in so great a State shall not be permitted to express their preferences on questions of this character, and that if they have clear and distinct preferences they shall be utterly helpless in the selection of the methods by which that preference is to be made effectual? It is absurd upon the face of it to say that Illinois or any other State, has the right to instruct its delegates to vote for a particular candidate, and yet has not the power to make such instructions effectual and binding.[7]

Speaking in favor of Rapier, Smith and Warner being seated, a Mr. Bateman of Ohio, a member of the rules committee, said the following:

Now, sir, we have the question presented whether this State convention, meeting in Montgomery – has the right not only to instruct a delegate how he shall vote, but, when he refuses to comply with their requirements, to remove him from his place and appoint another man in his stead without consulting the advice of the delegates representing that district.... The people of that district elected him as their representative to this Convention. That convention then required him to furnish them a pledge that he would vote as they wanted....

This letter was served upon Mr. Rapier... and Mr. Rapier treated it with that contempt which, in my judgement, it deserved.[8]

When the roll call was taken on whether to seat Rapier, Smith and Warner, the minority report endorsing the state's authority to bind delegates was rejected on a 306-449 vote, and appeals to deference for state party powers to ignore the national rules failed.

The fact that national rules trump state rules in the event of a conflict isn't simply an anachronistic legacy dating from a long-ago time period when the Republican Party had very different ideas on local versus national power. In recent years, whenever the question has been raised of whether state or national party rules take precedence, the national rules have always been found to be controlling.

While it is clear that national party rules take precedence over state rules, another question arises – what about state laws?

The first state law attempting to direct delegates in their vote appears to have been an Oregon ballot measure approved in November 1910, adding the presidential nomination process to the state's primary election law.[9] Several other states adopted similar laws, all due to the efforts of "Progressive Era" activists of the time who sought to expand the power and reach of the government.

According to an academic paper of the time, the Oregon law sought to "make the preferential vote binding by requiring every delegate to take an oath of office that he will 'to the best of his judgement and ability, faithfully carry out the wishes of his party as expressed by its voters at the time of his election.'"[10] But as discussed in Chapter 1, at the 1912, 1916, and 1920 Republican National Conventions, the Oregon primary instructions were ignored, and in two of the three instances, the convention chair polled the delegation when requested by a delegate, with each individual being free to vote his conscience. In 1916 there was no request to poll the delegation.

Maryland, North Dakota, and several other states enacted similar laws during the Progressive Era. At the 1920 convention, Maryland appears to have cast its votes in line with the state law on the first ballot, casting all 16 of its votes for Gen. Leonard Wood, and on every ballot until the 10th and final ballot, when delegates requested a poll of the delegation and split their votes between Wood, Ohio Sen. Warren Harding, and businessman Herbert Hoover.[11] North Dakota's delegation appears to have ignored its state law entirely, giving two votes to Wood and eight to California Sen. Hiram Johnson on the first ballot and continuing to split their votes among several candidates throughout the remaining ballots.[12]

Clearly, the efforts by state legislatures to bind delegates fared no better at the Republican National Convention than the efforts of state

parties. But following the 1968 Democratic convention and the reform effort coming from it, several more states passed laws requiring that delegates to national conventions vote according to the results of state primary contests, and the question again came up – could states bind delegates to national party conventions to vote according to primary results? As a series of court decisions in the 1970s and beyond made clear, the answer was still no – such laws are unconstitutional.

> **A series of court decisions in the 1970s and beyond made clear state laws that bind delegates to vote for a specific candidate are unconstitutional.**

Beginning in the late 1890s, courts around the country had begun to consider the degree to which the state could intrude on the internal matters of a political party. There was little doubt that in the case of laws directly involving the election of public officials, there was some necessary regulation and interaction between political parties and the state. For example, in *State v. Felton*, the Ohio Supreme Court upheld a legal requirement that parties had to have received 10 percent or more of the vote in the previous election in order to secure automatic ballot access.[13]

But as regards the internal matters of a party, such as election or selection of delegates to a national convention, the courts have generally found that, under the First Amendment's right of freedom of association, the state cannot intrude on such matters. The exceptions largely revolved around racial discrimination, such as the "White Primaries" that the Democratic Party in several Southern states had established during the Jim Crow era. In 1944, the U.S. Supreme Court ruling in *Smith v. Allwright* struck down the disenfranchisement of African-Americans in Democratic primaries:

> Primary elections are conducted by the party under state statutory authority. The county executive committee selects precinct election officials and the county, district or state executive committees, respectively, canvass the returns....

The state courts are given exclusive original jurisdiction of contested elections and of mandamus proceedings to compel party
officers to perform their statutory duties.

We think that this statutory system for the selection of party
nominees for inclusion on the general election ballot makes the
party which is required to follow these legislative directions an
agency of the state in so far as it determines the participants in a
primary election. The party takes its character as a state agency
from the duties imposed upon it by state statutes; the duties do not
become matters of private law because they are performed by a
political party....

Constitutional rights would be of little value if they could be thus
indirectly denied....[14]

The key factor that allowed the court to reach this decision, as the
excerpts above demonstrate, is that the activities of the Democratic Party
of Texas were considered to be state action because the party was determined by the court to be acting as an agent of the state.

The ability of the state to insert itself into internal party matters is
otherwise quite limited – as one scholar in this area notes, "The current
majority judicial position on state action and political parties appears to
depend greatly on whether racial or other 'invidious' discrimination is
present."[15]

Beginning with a relatively obscure opinion in Pennsylvania in 1963,
courts began to affirm that when it came to electing party officials, such
as county chairs or state central committee members, political parties
were free to do as they wish. In *Lynch v. Torquato* a voter challenged the
election of a Democratic Party county chair on equal protection grounds.
The federal district court judge denied the challenge, explaining that the
position of county chair was not a publicly elected position, nor did it hold
any public or quasi-public duties. His ruling was upheld by the Third
Circuit Court of Appeals in an opinion that largely echoed the lower
court's finding that the position of county chair was a private issue, not

public.[16] Later U.S. Supreme Court rulings embraced the *Lynch* reasoning.

The decisive ruling on the matter, at least as it relates to the state's ability to dictate to political parties on matters relating to delegates to national conventions, came in 1975, and arose out of a controversy at the 1972 Democratic National Convention.

In March 1972, the state of Illinois held a primary election for delegates to the Democratic National Convention. In that primary, a slate of 59 delegates controlled by Chicago Mayor Richard J. Daley was elected, later called the Wigoda delegation. A rival delegation, later called the Cousins delegation, was elected at private party caucuses held in June.

> "The States themselves have no constitutionally mandated role in the great task of the selection of the Presidential and Vice-Presidential candidates... Such a regime could seriously undercut or indeed destroy the effectiveness of the National Party Convention as a concerted enterprise engaged in the vital process of choosing Presidential and Vice-Presidential candidates."

Both delegations arrived at the Democratic National Convention, and the Cousins delegation challenged the credentials of the Wigoda delegation, claiming that it didn't meet the party's guidelines requiring certain racial and gender quotas. The credentials committee agreed with the challengers, and it unseated members of the Wigoda delegation in favor of the Cousins delegation. The Wigoda delegation sued, claiming that because its members had been elected under state law, they were entitled to be seated.

The case eventually wound up at the U.S. Supreme Court, and in the January 1975 *Cousins v. Wigoda* decision it held that state law could not intrude upon a matter so fundamental to a party's freedom of association as which delegates should be seated:

> The States themselves have no constitutionally mandated role in the great task of the selection of the Presidential and Vice-Presidential

candidates. If the qualifications and eligibility of delegation to the National Political Party Conventions were left to state law "each of the fifty states could establish the qualifications of its delegates to the various party conventions without regard to party policy, an obviously intolerable result." [internal citation omitted] Such a regime could seriously undercut or indeed destroy the effectiveness of the National Party Convention as a concerted enterprise engaged in the vital process of choosing Presidential and Vice-Presidential candidates....[17]

While the *Cousins* decision centered on the national party's freedom to decide which delegates to seat and which to reject, the implications for the binding of delegates is clear: if a state cannot even dictate that a national party accept the delegates elected in a state-run primary, it certainly is not able to dictate how any delegates that are seated should vote on the presidential nomination or any other issue.

This is not a disputed point. It was, in fact, the commonly held understanding at the Republican National Convention in 1976, the first such convention held after the *Cousins* decision. As discussed in Chapter 2, the whole point of the Justice Amendment pushed through the convention rules committee was to bind delegates to the outcome of primaries despite the fact that such laws had been nullified by the Supreme Court's decision.

Recall the words of Mr. Cramer, the general counsel to the Republican National Committee, at the 1976 convention explaining the need for a rule to bind the delegates:

> [B]ecause this convention, under *Cousins v. Wigoda*, regardless of the state law, would have license to do what it saw fit according to its party rules....
>
> I am saying that *Cousins v. Wigoda* in effect said that the party can do as it sees fit with regard to delegate selection matters, even though it is totally contrary to state law. We in fact are saying in this amendment that because of *Cousins v. Wigoda* ... delegates could, without this resolution, vote contrary to State law, that they shall be bound by state law.[18]

Any doubt about the accuracy of Cramer's understanding should have been eliminated following the 1983 U.S. Supreme Court decision in *Democratic Party of the United States v. Wisconsin ex rel. Le Follette,* a case directly implicating the binding of delegates to a national convention.

Wisconsin first enacted legislation in 1904 creating direct primary elections, and in 1911 it expanded its law to cover the presidential nomination process. In 1949 the law was amended to require that delegates to national conventions vote according to the outcome of the primary, and that law remained on the books through at least the 1980 nomination cycle.[19]

At the 1976 national convention the Democratic Party adopted rules limiting their nomination process to Democrats and specified that the binding of delegates according to primary results would only be permitted in primaries in which only Democrats could vote. Because Wisconsin held an "open" primary in which people who were not Democrats were allowed to vote, it risked having its delegation not seated at the 1980 convention. The Democratic Party of Wisconsin sued the national party to overturn the rule.[20]

The Wisconsin Supreme Court upheld the state's open primary and delegate binding law, but the U.S. Supreme Court overturned that decision, ruling that both the courts and state legislatures could have only a limited role in regulating political parties.[21] The decision cited the earlier *Cousins* decision as the controlling opinion, and was summarized in a law review article this way:

> The Court reasoned, to the extent the National Party chose to disregard open primary results as reflecting, at least in part, the will of persons unaffiliated with the Party, Wisconsin's attempt to require the National Party to accept delegates sworn to vote in accord with the open primary outcome interfered with the National Party's freedom of association.[22]

Delivering the majority opinion, Justice Potter Stewart wrote the following:

The voters in Wisconsin's "open" primary express their choice among Presidential candidates for the Democratic Party's nomination; they do not vote for delegates to the National Convention. Delegates to the National Convention are chosen separately, after the primary, at caucuses of persons who have stated their affiliation with the Party. But these delegates, under Wisconsin law, are bound to vote at the National Convention in accord with the results of the open primary election. Accordingly, while Wisconsin's open Presidential preference primary does not itself violate National Party rules, the State's mandate that the results of the primary shall determine the allocation of votes cast by the State's delegates at the National Convention does....

The question in this case is not whether Wisconsin may conduct an open primary election if it chooses to do so, or whether the National Party may require Wisconsin to limit its primary election to publicly declared Democrats. Rather, the question is whether, once Wisconsin has opened its Democratic Presidential preference primary to voters who do not publicly declare their party affiliation, it may then bind the National Party to honor the binding primary results, even though those results were reached in a manner contrary to National Party rules....

The State asserts a compelling interest in preserving the overall integrity of the electoral process, providing secrecy of the ballot, increasing voter participation in primaries, and preventing harassment of voters. But all those interests go to the conduct of the Presidential preference primary – not to the imposition of voting requirements upon those who, in a separate process, are eventually selected as delegates. Therefore, the interests advanced by the State do not justify its substantial intrusion into the associational freedom of members of the National Party....

The National Party rules do not forbid Wisconsin to conduct an open primary. But if Wisconsin does open its primary, it cannot require that Wisconsin delegates to the National Party Convention

vote there in accordance with the primary results, if to do so would violate Party rules.[23]

More recently, a federal district court in Florida relied upon the *Cousins v. Wigoda* decision in ruling against a Democratic operative who sued both the Democratic National Committee and the Florida Democratic Party in an attempt to force the national party to seat the Florida delegation at the national convention. The state had held its primary election in January, contrary to national party rules specifying that presidential contests could only be held between the first Tuesday in February and the second Tuesday in June, except for the states of Iowa, New Hampshire, Nevada and South Carolina. As a result, the national party had threatened not to seat the Florida delegation.

The judge rejected the plaintiff's claims against the state and national parties for a range of shortcomings, and in his October 2007 opinion noted the following:

> Finally ... the Supreme Court has consistently recognized that national political parties have a constitutionally protected right to manage and conduct their own internal affairs, including the enforcement of delegate selection rules and the decision as to which state delegates it will recognize, under the First Amendment's right to freedom of association, and that associational right generally prevails over any countervailing state interest or the interest of any individual voter.... In Lafollete, for example, the Supreme Court specifically stressed that "a State, or a court, may not constitutionally substitute its own judgment for that of the party.... The Court in LaFollette also observed that a state must demonstrate a "compelling" interest to warrant interference with the party's constitutionally-protected associational rights and that the State of Wisconsin had not met its burden of establishing such a compelling state interest.... [T]he Court cannot require Florida delegates to the Convention to vote there in accordance with the primary results where the primary violates the DNC's rules.[24]

The case was ultimately dismissed based on a lack of standing, but it is clear that the understanding of *Cousins* that was voiced in the rules committee meeting of the 1976 Republican National Convention remains the law of the land, and no state (or court) may reach into the internal affairs of a political party in a way that interferes with the selection of delegates, or whom those delegates may or may not vote for.

> "The Supreme Court has consistently recognized that national political parties have a constitutionally protected right to manage and conduct their own internal affairs, including the enforcement of delegate selection rules and the decision as to which state delegates it will recognize, under the First Amendment's right to freedom of association."

Between the rules as written and enforced at the Republican National Convention over the past 160 years rejecting efforts to bind delegates (with the exception of 1976), the supremacy of national party rules over state party rules, and a string of court decisions affirming the constitutional right of political parties to be free of state intrusion, it's clear that Republican delegates at the national convention remain free to vote their conscience on all matters that come up for a vote, at least so long as the Garfield language is present in the standing rules of the convention and there are no changes similar to the Justice Amendment of 1976. The next chapter addresses the question: Is this a good thing?

---

[1] Rimel, A. (2016, April 17). Primary education: How Oregon blazed the way for primary elections. Corvallis Gazette-Times.

[2] Jackson, J.S. (2015). The American Political Party System. The Brookings Institution, 66-67,

[3] Becker, C. (1899, October). The Unit Rule in National Nominating Conventions. The American Historical Review 5(1), 82.

[4] The challenge to the Alabama and Illinois delegates also involved the matter of "district representation," the idea that each congressional district in any given state was entitled to

send the delegates it wished to the national convention. Thus it would be inaccurate to say that the matter of binding delegates was solely at issue in these credentials cases. But the critical lesson of these credentials challenges was that when state practices and rules conflict with national rules, the national rules take precedence.

5 Proceedings of the Republican National Convention (1880), 46-47.

6 Ibid., 51.

7 Ibid., 58.

8 Ibid., 89.

9 Rimel, A. (2016, April 17). Primary education: How Oregon blazed the way for primary elections. Corvallis Gazette-Times.

10 Aylsworth, L.E. (1912, August). Presidential Primary Elections — Legislation of 1910-1912. The American Political Science Review 6(3), 433.

11 Proceedings of the 1920 Republican National Convention, 21.

12 Ibid., 184-220.

13 Wigton, R.C. (2014). The Parties in Court. Lexington Books, 7.

14 U.S. Supreme Court ruling in Smith v. Allwright, 321 U.S. 649 (1944).

15 Ibid at note xii, p. 26.

16 Ibid., 79-80.

17 U.S. Supreme Court ruling in Cousins v. Wigoda, 419 U.S. 477 (1975).

18 Transcript of the rules committee of the Republican National Convention (1976), 265.

19 Geyh, C.G. (1983). "It's My Party and I'll Cry If I Want To": State Intrusions upon the Associational Freedoms of Political Parties – Democratic Party of the United States v. Wisconsin ex rel. La Follette. Wisconsin Law Review, 212, 214.

20 Ibid., 215.

21 Ibid. at note xii, 115.

22 Ibid. at note xix, 218.

23 Supreme Court opinion in Democratic Party of the United States v. Wisconsin ex rel. Le Follette (1981), 450 U.S. 107.

24 Order of Richard Lazzara, United States District Judge, Middle District of Florida, Victor Dimaio v. Democratic National Committee and Florida Democratic Party. (2007, Oct. 5), 9-10

Chapter 5 –
Why Should Delegates Be Unbound?

The previous four chapters showed conclusively that delegates to the Republican National Convention have always, with the exception of 1976, been free to vote their consciences on all matters before the convention, including the nomination of the party's candidate for president of the United States. But is it healthy for the Republican Party, and for the nation as a whole, if delegates are not bound to the results of primary and caucus votes? After all, our country is supposed to be founded on democratic ideals, where the votes of the people are supposed to be the supreme authority on political matters.

For a variety of reasons, the answer is yes, it is healthy for the party and the nation if convention delegates are free to exercise their individual judgment and conscience when it comes to their vote at the Republican National Convention.

It's worth stepping back for a moment to consider several qualifications to the idea that America is a democratic nation. It is indisputably true in the sense that as a foundational principle, legitimate government authority in the United States comes from the people as a whole and cannot be exercised without the consent of the governed.

But the United States is not a direct democracy. Instead, it is typically characterized as a democratic republic, or representative democracy. Both terms mean that individual citizens elect representatives not to execute specified instructions, but to mediate and consider issues on their behalf and then direct specific actions. This is how Congress and the 50 state legislatures operate. Indeed, it is how most deliberative bodies in America are run.

The Republican National Convention operates as a deliberative body, with delegates to the national convention arriving as a result of elections and selections according to a variety of processes. Some states elect delegates directly by name on primary ballots, some are appointed by the state party's leadership, and still others begin the process by being elected at local precinct caucuses until finally they are elected at a district or state convention.

Whatever the process, they arrive at the convention with a clear purpose of representing the interests and preferences of their constituents and of exercising their judgment in how to best do so. It is impossible to exercise such judgment if the result has been predetermined on any question and the delegate's role is simply to show up to rubber-stamp the decision handed to him or her. Delegates to the national convention are not members of a Supreme Soviet in a communist dictatorship, where their job is to ratify other's decisions and applaud at the appropriate times. As the preceding chapters demonstrate, the rules of the Republican National Convention have historically pre-vented the imposition of pre-deter-mined results on roll call votes, at least if delegates chose to avail themselves of the conscience protec-tions.

> **Delegates to the national convention are not members of a Supreme Soviet in a communist dictatorship, where their job is to ratify other's decisions and applaud at the appropriate times.**

On most matters that come before the convention, this is not a disputed point. Few would argue today that delegates can be effectively bound on votes affecting whether to accept the credentials committee report,[1] or on adjournment, or on any matter other than the balloting for the party's nomination for president. And even that supposed binding (for presidential voting) only extends so far in most cases – most state party rules or state laws that purport to bind delegates only do so for the first ballot, and if additional ballots are needed, most delegate instructions then acknowledge that delegates are free to vote their consciences.[2]

As a practical matter, the lifting of instructions of delegates after a first ballot is necessary because without it, nearly all delegates would ostensibly be required to vote as before, resulting in an unbreakable cycle of ballots with no selection of a nominee. So even if binding were enforce-able under the rules, it could only be acknowledged as an exception to the general principle that delegates are free to vote according to their own consciences.

However, just because delegates have the freedom to vote their consciences at the convention, it doesn't mean they should do so lightly if

it is in conflict with other obligations and pledges they may have assumed. At the 1964 convention rules committee meeting, during the discussion of whether to add language explicitly prohibiting the unit rule, a Mr. Ross offered the following comments:

> I have discussed this suggestion with several other people who believe that the adoption of this change in the rule and the atten-dant publicity which would be given to it would convince some delegates they are released not only from a legal obligation which they never had but also from a moral obligation which some of them do have. This includes Nebraska. Nebraska has several delegates who have signed written pledges in order to get their names put on in a certain way they will support a certain candidate. If this is the effect, the publicity given to this rule change … would tend to give the delegates they no longer have a moral responsibil-ity to the state convention or to the people who elected them, then I think probably we should not go ahead and pass the change in the resolution.[3]

Even though the 1964 convention could not have enforced the pledges the Nebraska delegates had signed, it should be obvious that delegates who break such a pledge and cast their votes for another candidate ought to be ready to explain their decisions to those to whom they made the pledge. And when they return home, they must be prepared to accept that if their reasons are found unsatisfactory then they are unlikely to be trusted with the honor of being delegates again, or enjoying any other positions of trust within the party. Exercising one's conscience is not a get-out-of-jail-free card for delegates, and if doing so entails consequences, then they should be prepared to bear them.

This, then, is another similarity between a delegate elected to the national convention and a representative or senator elected to Congress.

> **Just because delegates have the freedom to vote their consciences at the convention, it doesn't mean they should do so lightly if it is in conflict with other obligations and pledges they may have assumed.**

Candidates who pledge to oppose tax increases, for instance, are likely to have to explain any votes to raise taxes when they return to their constituents. But any such pledge is not legally enforceable,[4] and the elected official may well have a plausible or even acceptable reason for breaking the pledge, such as tolerating a small tax increase in order to achieve a bigger, more important policy victory, such as taxing corporate welfare in order to reduce government giveaways to favored industries.

Let's examine some of the circumstances under which a delegate pledged to vote for a particular candidate might make the judgment on the floor of the convention that he cannot reconcile his conscience with his pledge, or accept any binding forced upon him by state party rule or state law. One such circumstance would be the case of a candidate that is dramatically out of step with the principles and values of the Republican Party.

Two statements in past conventions stand out in support of the idea that a delegate shouldn't be forced to vote for a candidate that does not meaningfully reflect or represent the values of the Republican Party, both of which appeared in earlier chapters.

In 1876, when debating whether four Pennsylvania delegates should have their votes recorded as they wished or whether the unit rule should be enforced, Mr. Woodford of New York made the following comments:

> I believe that under the very existence alike of the nation and the Republican party, is the right of every man to cast his own vote.... I love the Republican party for the ideas of the party, and not for the form and the deadness of its organization. I want to say another thing, for silence here were crime. As an honorable man I am bound, as honorable men you're bound, to abide the actions of the convention; but should this or any convention make declaration of unworthy principles, or place thereon candidates whose lives and records do not represent what true Republicanism means, then let me to-day and here simply say, in words so plain that none may misunderstand, I am bound to my country and its welfare by a higher tie than that which binds me to the Republican party.[5]

And as noted in Chapter 2, at the 1980 convention rules committee meeting when the discussion turned to eliminating the Justice Amendment language and returning to the past practice of allowing all delegates to vote their consciences, Mr. Beard of North Carolina offered the following observation:

> [I]f we do not delete 18(a) language.... I believe the people of Illinois, of Massachusetts, of Connecticut, and of possibly New Hampshire, will find themselves in the envious position at this Convention of casting their votes for a left-wing lunatic by the name of John Anderson. I would not impose that burden upon the conscience of any Republican.[6]

More ominously, consider the case of former Ku Klux Klan leader David Duke, who ran as a candidate for the Republican nomination in 1992. While he did poorly in nearly every contest, he did receive 10.6 percent of the vote in Mississippi, 8.9 percent in Louisiana, and 7.1 percent in South Carolina.

While those numbers didn't result in his being allocated any delegates in those states, it's possible and even likely that without Pat Buchanan's challenge to President George H.W. Bush, Duke would have captured a larger share of the vote. This is based on the assumption that turnout would have been lower without Buchanan's high-profile campaign against Bush[7] and that Duke's positions would have enabled him in those three states to draw roughly similar numbers of voters as well as possibly some of the Buchanan protest voters. With Duke as the sole alternative to Bush in those three states, particularly Louisiana where he had been the GOP nominee for governor just months earlier, Duke conceivably would have received 15 or 20 percent or more of the vote in these states.

Needless to say, requiring a delegate to the Republican National Convention to honor any allocation and binding process that might force them to vote for a former Ku Klux Klan leader would be an intolerable infringement on any decent person's conscience, not to mention a national embarrassment for the GOP.

While the Duke scenario above is hypothetical, the Democrats have in fact faced similar scenarios at recent national conventions. In 1996,

convicted felon and perennial fringe candidate Lyndon LaRouche garnered enough primary votes in Louisiana and Virginia to be awarded one pledged delegate from each state, and in 2012 another perennial fringe candidate and incarcerated felon, Keith Russell Judd, received 40 percent of the vote against Obama in the 2012 West Virginia Democratic primary, which would have entitled him to about a dozen delegates under the party's proportional allocation system.[8]

> **Requiring a delegate to the Republican National Convention to honor any allocation and binding process that might force them to vote for a former Ku Klux Klan leader would be an intolerable infringement on any decent person's conscience.**

In both cases the Democrats avoided further embarrassment by relying on party rules to refuse to seat or allocate delegates to the two fringe candidates. But the implications are obvious: Primaries can on occasion produce results that, were the binding of delegates enforced, would require some delegates to vote for an appalling choice.

Another reason why a delegate might reconsider or repudiate any pledge or purported binding is that circumstances may change. When new knowledge about candidates is uncovered between the primary and the time the delegates must cast their vote on the convention floor, some leeway becomes necessary.

Consider the case of John Edwards, former U.S. senator from North Carolina and two-time candidate for the Democratic presidential nomination. Following his selection as the Democrats' vice-presidential nominee in 2004, Edwards was considered one of the major contenders for his party's 2008 nomination. After finishing second in the Iowa caucuses, he fell to third in New Hampshire and dropped out several weeks later following disappointing results in South Carolina and Florida.

At the time of his campaign, Edwards was having an affair with another woman and fathered a child with her while his wife was receiving treatment for cancer. The affair had been revealed by a *National Enquirer* article before the Iowa caucuses, but Edwards denied the allegations and an extensive cover-up effort seemed to put the issue to rest. In late July

2008, however, Edwards was found by media at the same hotel as his mistress and their child, and two weeks later he admitted to the affair.

But imagine that things had played out somewhat differently – that Edwards had continued his campaign past Florida's January 29 primary and done well enough to at least play "kingmaker" by not releasing the delegates pledged to him at the Democratic National Convention, promising to throw his support behind either President Barack Obama or former Secretary of State Hillary Clinton to clinch their nomination with delegates committed to him,[9] or even that he had managed to do well enough to be the presumptive nominee. But also imagine in this scenario that the confirmation and admission of Edwards' affair still happened on the same dates as they did in real life, just weeks before the Democratic National Convention was scheduled to begin on August 25.

Assuming Edwards failed to release his delegates (after all, Bill Clinton had survived infidelity allegations during his campaign as well as his presidency, so Edwards might well have thought he could press on), should his delegates have been bound to vote for him? Should their earlier pledges of support be held against them, or would it be reasonable instead for any delegate pledged to Edwards to announce their renunciation of the pledge in light of what had been revealed?

This is obviously a hypothetical, but revelations (or the anticipation of possible revelations) about candidates that might reasonably cause a pledged delegate to reconsider his or her commitment are hardly unknown. For example, in the 2016 campaign, Hillary Clinton seemed the likely Democratic nominee, but an indictment over the mishandling of classified information would almost certainly cause some of her pledged delegates to want to vote for someone else.

Should Clinton actually be indicted, the Democrats do have conscience protections of their own for their delegates that would allow them to exercise their judgment and ignore their pledges. Rule 12(J) of the Democratic National Convention for 2016 states the following:

> Delegates elected to the national convention pledged to a presidential candidate shall in all good conscience reflect the sentiments of those who elected them.

The same rule was in effect in 2008, and at that time a Democratic Party spokesperson released a statement explaining the party's position on "pledged" and "bound" delegates:

> Under the Democratic Party's Rules, pledged delegates are not legally "bound" or required to vote according to their presidential preference on the first ballot at the Convention....
>
> A delegate goes to the Convention with a signed pledge of support for a particular presidential candidate. At the Convention, while it is assumed that the delegate will cast their vote for the candidate they are publicly pledged to, it is not required. Under the Delegate Selection Rules, a delegate is asked to "in good conscience reflect the sentiments of those who elected them." This provision is designed in part to make the Convention a deliberative body. Delegates are not bound to vote for the candidate they are pledged to at the Convention or on the first ballot.[10]

In addition to freeing delegates from being forced to vote for an indicted candidate, this rule would also have protected delegates from being bound to vote for LaRouche in 1996 or Judd in 2012, and the language reflects the Democratic Party's decision following 1968 to emulate the Republican Party's longstanding tradition of respecting and protecting the conscience rights of delegates.

The ability of delegates to the Republican National Convention to vote their conscience also helps to ensure that the affairs of the Republican Party are controlled by Republicans, and not by outsiders who may have little interest in protecting the viability, principles, and relevance of the party and are instead simply attempting to co-opt the party for other purposes.

Voters in Republican primaries and caucuses may or may not be Republicans, especially in states that permit same-day party registration (sometimes followed by immediate de-registration after casting a ballot) or hold open primaries in which any citizen may select the party in which they wish to vote. While there is value in seeing the preferences of independent or only marginally affiliated Republicans, in that it can provide a

sense of how particular candidates might fare in a general election matchup, it would be a mistake to assume that "Republicans for a day" should be given the same weight in shaping the party as committed Republicans, such as elected delegates who typically are long-serving and proven party members with a strong commitment to the well-being of the party.[11]

Deferring to the judgment of delegates is not the same as deferring to so-called party "insiders." Because delegate election processes typically begin at the grassroots level and conclude at district or state conventions, it's actually more likely that the activist base of the party will be well represented in the delegation instead of simply being stocked with supposed insiders.

A study within the past few years of delegates to past Republican National Conventions support the idea that delegates are unlikely simply be party insiders. Over the past several decades, "Republicans have had a fairly high rate of turnover in their national conventions."[12] The number of delegates attending their first national convention has routinely been at or above 60 percent,[13] which would not be the case if the party were regularly turning to the same group of party insiders.

Also, delegates to the national convention are generally more conservative on issues like the size of government, defense spending, and abortion than Republicans overall.[14] In surveys dating to 1972, Republican delegates have become increasingly more conservative. At the 2008 convention, the most recent for which there is data available, 81 percent of Republican delegates described themselves as conservative, while in 1972 only 57 percent of delegates described themselves that way.[15] All of these points would seem to further discredit the idea that "insider" delegates, drawn from moderate or "establishment" elites, might foist a moderate nominee upon the party.

A look at almost any delegation to the Republican National Convention will show it to be a mix of people who have a wide range of backgrounds – many of them are longtime party loyalists and issue activists who toil year in and year out to build the party and conservative movement by serving as county chairs, volunteering for campaigns at all levels, or leading grassroots organizations supporting conservative causes. These are the individuals that the Republican Party has for 160 years entrusted

with the responsibility of exercising their judgment and conscience in determining the party's nominee.

Another reason delegates need to be free to vote according to their own judgment is that it may become obvious a particular candidate is unable to mount a competitive, credible and competent campaign. While nobody can predict with absolute certainty whether a potential presidential nominee will be a good candidate, delegates to the national convention are generally politically astute people who are likely to recognize the traits of a candidate that are seriously incompatible with the ability to mount a successful campaign.

Reasonable people will disagree over what those traits might be – some might argue that simply receiving the largest number of votes in the primaries and caucuses is sufficient proof of political competence and competitiveness, while others might consider factors like high disapproval numbers or past statements and actions likely to repel large numbers of voters.

But in recent years Republicans have seen candidates go from competitive or even favored to unelectable based on a careless statement – U.S. Senate candidates Todd Akin of Missouri and Richard Mourdock of Indiana arguably lost winnable races in 2012 due to inarticulate statements regarding rape and abortion, and it's possible a future presumptive Republican nominee might likewise make statements that are so damaging to not only their candidacy but also to the party's brand and the election prospects of other Republicans running that year that some delegates might be unwilling to vote for what they view as a certain defeat likely to inflict long-term disaster on the party.

> **The party's conscience protections for delegates can serve, then, as a final check on what might otherwise be an impending electoral disaster for the party.**

The party's conscience protections for delegates can serve, then, as a final check on what might otherwise be an impending electoral disaster for the party. It's easy to envision a scenario in which one candidate collects enough delegates to become the presumptive nominee of the party, but before the convention he or she engages in behavior or

makes statements that all but guarantee a crushing defeat in the general election. In such a scenario, should the delegates be forced to effectively cede the presidency because of votes cast before under different circumstances?

This chapter has presented a broad range of arguments in support of the Republican Party's longstanding freedom of delegates to vote their consciences in all matters that come before the convention. It should be clear that the existing rules serve the Republican Party and the Republican National Convention far better than any requirement that delegates rubber-stamp a decision made months ago, especially when new facts or circumstances have arisen indicating that adhering to the earlier decision would damage the party and the nation.

---

[1] At the 1912 convention, during a roll call of the states regarding credentials, the chair of the North Carolina delegation announced that a resolution had been passed instructing him that on all matters the delegation was to vote 23-1 in favor of the position of the Roosevelt forces, and subsequently voted 1-23 on a motion regarding the seating of pro-Taft delegates. Another delegate challenged the announcement, a poll of the delegation was called, and the final vote from North Carolina was recorded as two "yea" and 22 "nay." See Proceedings of the 1912 Republican National Convention, 154.

[2] Taylor, J. (2016, April 17). Here's A Round-By-Round Guide To A Contested GOP Convention. NPR.

[3] Transcript of the 1964 Republican National Convention rules committee meeting. 66 – 67.

[4] Standler, R. B. (2012, April 29). Promises by Political Candidates Not Legally Enforceable in the USA. www.rbs2.com.

[5] Proceedings of the 1876 Republican National Convention. 97.

[6] Transcript of the 1980 Republican National Convention rules committee meeting. 63.

[7] Bipartisan Policy Center. (2012, October) National Primary Turnout Hits Record Low, summary charts, 1. Shows that the 1972, 1984 and 2004 Republican turnout percentages in uncontested nominations were lower than contested nomination fights in 1988, 1996, 2000, 2008, and 2012. Based on author's calculations of the Bipartisan Policy Center's data, turnout is roughly 31 percent lower in Republican presidential primaries that are uncontested.

[8] According to the website www.thegreenpapers.com, West Virginia was to allocate 36 delegates according to congressional district and statewide primary results – depending on the exact formula used, Judd could have expected to receive between 12 and 14 delegates.

[9] Obama had 1,766.5 delegates pledged to him as a result of Democratic primary and caucus results, compared to Clinton's 1,639.5. Edwards finished with 21 pledged delegates, which

went to Obama following Edwards' endorsement. On the actual roll call, Clinton released her delegates to vote as they wished, and many of them voted for Obama.

[10] E-mail from Stacy Paxton, Democratic National Committee press secretary, to Anna Marie Cox, "Pledged delegates vs. 'bound' delegates," Time, February 19, 2008.

[11] Jackson, J. S. (2015). The American Political Party System. Brookings Institution, 156.

[12] Ibid., 154.

[13] Ibid., 149.

[14] Ibid., 116-147. In 2008, 74 percent of Republican delegates favored a government that provided fewer services than at present, compared with only 41 percent of self-identified Republicans. Delegates were also more conservative on every other issue reported, including favoring private health insurance solutions over government insurance (87-55), increases in defense spending (87-59), and bans on all or most abortions (88-70).

[15] Ibid., 93

Chapter 6 –
Responding to Objections

In the previous five chapters, we have read (1) a detailed history in support of the assertion that all delegates at the Republican National Convention have always been free (in 39 out of 40 conventions) to vote their own judgment in all matters before them, and (2) the arguments in favor of retaining this freedom for delegates. So long as the language of what is now Rule 37 (b) of the temporary standing rules of the 2016 convention remains in place, or at least is not substantially changed, delegates to the upcoming convention will likewise enjoy the same freedom as almost all of their predecessors.

While the evidence for these conclusions is overwhelming, it is not universally accepted – other interpretations challenge part or all of the conclusions offered here. With that in mind, Chapter 6 will examine and respond to a few of the more common objections to these conclusions. These claims largely have been presented in either media outlets, Republican National Committee or Republican National Convention rules committee meetings, or comments and memos from the office of the Republican National Committee's legal counsel. Several of these objections have been addressed in previous chapters but are also summarized here.

Objection 1: This would disenfranchise millions of people who vote in primaries, whose votes are now "worthless" if delegates can vote however they please.

It is true that without the binding of delegates, the votes of primary voters and caucus attendees is somewhat diminished compared with how delegate allocation and binding is often interpreted. But that is a far cry from saying that they are worthless or that voters have been disenfranchised.

Primaries that do not bind delegates will still signal to delegates which candidates are able to draw supporters to the polls. For example, when Sen. Eugene McCarthy finished with a better-than-expected second-place finish in the 1968 New Hampshire primary, it sent a signal to Democrats

that incumbent President Lyndon Johnson would be a weak candidate, prompting him to drop out of the race. In 1952 a loss in the New Hampshire primary to Tennessee Sen. Estes Kefauver likewise pushed President Harry Truman out of the race. This was despite the fact that in both cases the New Hampshire primary was understood to be simply a "beauty contest."

The results of primaries and caucuses held across the nation are, and will remain, an important consideration for delegates considering how to cast their vote. But retaining the protections of Rule 37 (b) for delegates to ensure they are free to vote for the presidential nominee allows for additional considerations to be brought in, including how well potential nominees reflect Republican principles and whether they can mount a credible campaign for the general election.

Objection 2: The rules cited, 37 (b) and 38, are modified or overridden by other parts of the rules that implicitly endorse or explicitly require the binding of delegates.

Under the Republican Party's rules governing the convening of the 2016 convention, adopted at and following the 2012 convention, binding of delegates is mentioned multiple times in several rules governing the election and selection of delegates. More importantly, Rule 16 (a) (2) states the following:

The Secretary of the Convention shall faithfully announce and record each delegate's vote in accordance with the delegate's obligation under these rules, state law or state party rule. If any delegate bound by these rules, state party rule or state law to vote for a presidential candidate at the national convention demonstrates support under Rule 40 for any person other than the candidate to whom he or she is bound, such support shall not be recognized.

The language here is similar to the Justice Amendment inserted by the Gerald Ford campaign in 1976 as part of its effort to block Ronald Reagan from the nomination. But as discussed in Chapter 3, Rule 16 (a) (2) is not part of the temporary rules of the 2016 convention, and unless this or functionally similar language is inserted into the permanent rules for 2016, it will not be in force. Even if this or similar language is re-

tained in its current section on convening the following convention (in 2020), it will still not be in effect for the 2016 convention, because those rules pertain only to a future convention.

Also, just as Congress today cannot bind a future Congress, one convention cannot bind a future convention in terms of the rules it adopts. There is no credible argument that the Republican National Convention of 2012 could have adopted enforceable rules regarding the convention of 2016 – each convention is allowed to establish its own rules, including whether to accept and enforce the binding of delegates.

> **Just as Congress today cannot bind a future Congress, one convention cannot bind a future convention – each convention is allowed to establish its own rules, including whether to accept and enforce the binding of delegates.**

Objection 3: These delegate conscience protection rules were written and adopted more than a century ago, and can't be interpreted today the way they were in the distant past.

Today's Rule 37 (b) is remarkably identical to the original written by James Garfield in 1880, and that rule in turn has clear roots in previous rules written for conventions dating back to the first one, in 1856. But the meaning of the rule has remained the same throughout the ages, just as the general form and processes of the Republican National Convention have remained remarkably identical.

The first convention in 1856 was something of an ad hoc affair, understandably so. But consider the second convention, which led to the nomination of Abraham Lincoln. The proceedings included the election of a permanent chair; establishment of committees for credentials, rules (called Order of Business), permanent organization, and platform and resolutions; use of the rules of the U.S. House of Representatives for convention business, except where convention rules overrode them; and a schedule that required the nomination of candidates for president and vice

president to occur after the reports of the committee on platform and resolutions.

An attendee at that 1860 convention arriving at the 2016 convention would have little trouble following the proceedings, and the reverse is true as well. Just as the meaning of the rule from 1860 stipulating the use of the rules of the U.S. House of Representatives has not changed in the intervening years, neither has the meaning of the conscience protections long embedded in the rules of the Republican National Convention.

In addition, while Rule 37 (b) traces its origins to 1856 and the language adopted in 1880 is little changed over the past 136 years, the interpretation has remained constant throughout that time. Although there does not appear to be any invocation of delegate conscience protections in the past several conventions, it has been invoked as recently as 1976 on the presidential nomination, when a Virginia delegate requested a poll of the delegation.

And of course, if the interpretation of the rule had somehow changed over the past century and a half, the Ford campaign would not have wanted or needed to change the rule via the Justice Amendment at the 1976 convention. The Garfield language and its predecessors unquestionably meant exactly the same thing from 1856 through 1980, raising the question of when it might have changed so drastically as to be out of force by 2016 or earlier.

> **In a year in which the Republican Party and conservatives in particular honor the legacy of the late Supreme Court Justice Antonin Scalia, it would be a curious break from his views on the interpretation of laws to say that, regardless of what Rule 37 (b) meant from the time it was adopted until within recent memory, it now means something wholly different.**

Finally, in a year in which the Republican Party and conservatives in particular honor the legacy of the late Supreme Court Justice Antonin Scalia, it would be a curious break from his views on the interpretation of laws to say that, regardless of what Rule 37 (b) meant from the time it was

adopted until within recent memory, it now means something wholly different.

Objection 4: These rules apply only to "unit voting," and not to binding of delegates through state party rules or state law.

Rule 38 is in fact exclusively concerned with unit voting, which was defined in the permanent rules for the 2012 convention (and temporary rules of the 2016 convention) as a rule or law "under which a delegation at the national convention casts its entire vote as a unit as determined by a majority vote of the delegation." Delegation votes under the unit rule are by definition unanimous.

But as the first several chapters of the book document extensively, the anti-binding language was added in 1880 with an aim toward not just blocking the unit rule, but protecting the right of all delegates to cast their votes as they please. The discussion and debate at the 1876 and 1880 conventions where this issue was settled make it abundantly clear that *any* effort to bind a delegate's vote was unconscionable and would not be upheld by the Republican National Convention. The unit rule was the most common tool at that time for forcing delegates' votes to be reported a certain way regardless of their true wishes, but the rule that was adopted was not a simple prohibition on the unit rule, which would have been easy enough to write. Rather, it was a requirement that the delegation chair accurately announce the votes of the delegation, combined with a mechanism for individual delegates to challenge the announced vote.

Further proof of the fact that the conscience protections embedded in the Garfield language were not only intended to be applied to the unit rule can be found in the proceedings of the 1884 and 1888 conventions. Coming on the heels of the 1876 and 1880 conventions where the subject of protecting delegates' freedom to vote as they wish was extensively discussed and debated, the 1884 and 1888 conventions demonstrate amply what the understanding of the rule was during this time period.

As the proceedings of those two conventions document, the conscience protections embedded in the Garfield language were invoked on a total of 68 occasions in these two conventions.[1] Forty-nine of those occasions followed a split announcement by the delegation chair, in which

two or more candidates were initially reported as receiving votes from the delegation. If the convention rule were to be used only to prevent the unit rule from being invoked, then it would not have been invoked in these cases because the announced vote was not unanimous.

Objection 5: Retaining the conscience protections would lead to chaos at conventions as unbound delegates could vote for anyone they please, regardless of any pledge they made.

Although delegates arrive unbound at the convention, that does not mean they can do as they like without consequence. As discussed in Chapter 5, a delegate that has pledged her support to a particular candidate is going to have to think long and hard before breaking that pledge. Upon returning home, she will have to explain her decision, and if her answer is unsatisfactory, she is unlikely to enjoy much of a future in the Republican Party. After all, who would support for county chair, or state central committee, or national delegate, any person who has already broken a pledge for a non-legitimate reason?

And even in 1976, when Ford's campaign pushed through a rule change to bind delegates from 18 or 19 states, it is unlikely that without such a rule the outcome would have changed. Aside from Mississippi's use of the unit rule and the delegations bound by the Justice Amendment, every other delegate at the convention was free to vote his or her conscience, and nearly all stuck with their pledges. According to *Reagan's Revolution: The Untold Story of the Campaign That Started It All*, the binding of delegates likely only prevented the defection of 25 to 35 delegates – nearly all of the delegates pledged to Ford were

> According to *Reagan's Revolution: The Untold Story of the Campaign That Started It All*, the binding of delegates likely only prevented the defection of 25 to 35 delegates – nearly all of the delegates pledged to Ford were expected to vote for him even without the binding, and the same for those pledged to Reagan.

expected to vote for him even without the binding, and the same for those pledged to Reagan.[2]

As the 1964 rules committee meeting discussed, delegates do have a "moral responsibility" to vote according to their pledges, a responsibility that is not to be taken lightly. It is not difficult to imagine circumstances in which a delegate feels he cannot in good conscience vote for the candidate to which he is pledged – perhaps the candidate was indicted for a crime, or announced as a vice presidential nominee someone dramatically out of step with Republican principles (for instance, Arizona Sen. John McCain in 2008 was considering Democrat-turned-Independent Sen. Joseph Lieberman of Connecticut as his running mate), or otherwise demonstrated that he or she is unfit to be the nominee.

So while there may be a small number of delegates who fail to take their responsibilities seriously and break pledges for trivial reasons, the overwhelming number of them understand the gravity of their pledges and will break them in only the most dire and unusual of circumstances.

Objection 6: This may be how it was done in the past, but in recent conventions these conscience protections have not been asserted or utilized and are essentially a "dead letter."

While it is true that the specific mechanism for protecting the freedom of delegates to vote their consciences (i.e., a delegate challenge to an announced vote during a roll call of the states) does not appear to have been invoked since the 1976 convention (and not on the presidential nomination in that year), there are instances in which that freedom has been implicitly recognized since then.

For example, at the 2008 and 2012 conventions, delegates from several states had their votes announced as being in support of Ron Paul, despite the fact that those votes were out of step with the supposed binding imposed on them by either state law or state party rule. In the official proceedings of the Republican National Convention, the votes announced for Paul were not recorded for the candidate to which they were supposedly bound – they simply were not recorded because Paul had not been officially nominated. If the Republican National Convention by either 2008 or 2012 had determined that the conscience protections were

no longer in force, it would have recorded those Paul votes for whichever candidate they were bound to.

Also, given that each convention passes its own rules and can drop any obsolete or inapplicable language at the beginning, it would not make sense to declare a rule passed only days earlier to be a "dead letter" that cannot or will not be enforced.

---

[1] See Appendix C.

[2] Shirley, C. Reagan's Revolution: The Untold Story of the Campaign that Started it All, 307.

Chapter 7 –
Conclusions

In 1856, a new political party gathered in Philadelphia, intent on nominating a candidate who would carry its message of freedom into the presidential election against the Democratic Party's nominee, James Buchanan. Foremost on every delegate's mind was the issue of slavery, primarily its expansion into the Kansas territory.

But those delegates were not simply there to rubber-stamp decisions without giving their own consideration to what was before them. As the chairman of the Republican National Committee, Edwin D. Morgan of New York, explained in the very first address to the first Republican National Convention, delegates were there to direct the national party and were to rely upon their own conscience in doing so.

> Delegates of the Convention, Representatives of the Heart and the Hope of the Nation…. You are assembled for patriotic purposes. High expectations are cherished by the people. You are here to-day to give direction to a movement which is to decide whether the people of the United States are to be hereafter and forever chained to the present national policy of the extension of human slavery… Such is the magnitude of the question submitted. In its consideration, let us avoid all extremes – plant ourselves firmly on the Platform of the Constitution and the Union, taking no position which does not commend itself to the judgment of our consciences, our country, and of mankind. Of the wisdom of such a policy there need be no doubt; against which there can be no successful resistance.[1]

Given Morgan's statement to the assembled delegates, it should come as little surprise that from that first convention through the next 40, with a single exception, the Republican National Convention has historically recognized the freedom of every delegate to vote his conscience and, if he so chooses, ignore the efforts of candidates, state parties and state laws to force him to vote contrary to his own best judgment.

In fact, it would be odd if this were not the case. The Republican National Convention is understood to be the highest governing body for the Republican Party. Any issue that is contested at the convention is settled by a vote of delegates, whether the issue is simply whether to adjourn to a later time, approve or amend the convention rules, or whom to nominate as the party's candidate for president.

Most crucially to the point raised in this book, any dispute over the interpretation or application of the convention rules is ultimately to be settled by the delegates – the convention chair can make a ruling guided by precedent, advice from legal counsel, or whim, but all such rulings are subject to an appeal, which is to be decided by a simple majority of delegates.[2]

Given that delegates to the national convention hold the authority to decide all matters relating to the rules, and settle all disputes over the interpretation and application of those rules, it would make no sense to say that they can be bound in any meaningful manner – any binding that might be voted in by the delegates, such as happened in 1976, can just as easily be voted out by those same delegates, and any ruling from the chair attempting to bind them can be reversed by the delegates as well.

> **Any binding that might be voted in by the delegates, such as happened in 1976, can just as easily be voted out by those same delegates, and any ruling from the chair attempting to bind them can be reversed by the delegates as well.**

For the first 20 years of the party, the freedom of delegates to vote their consciences was generally accepted, although less explicit than it would later be. These early assertions of the right to vote according to conscience, such as the Pennsylvania delegates in 1868 challenging the unit rule, were made despite the absence of an explicit way to exercise it.

At the 1880 convention, this changed, with the addition of the language developed by James Garfield that spelled out a procedure for individual delegates to contest the announced vote by their delegation's chair. While the unit rule was at that time the main tool that could be used to deny delegates their freedom to vote as they wished, the extensive debate and discussion at the 1876 and 1880 conventions made clear that any effort to announce or record delegate votes contrary to their wishes would not be upheld. The fact that the delegate conscience protections were intended to extend beyond the unit rule can be seen in the first two conventions after the Garfield language was added, when 49 of the 68 invocations of the conscience protections followed instances in which the announced vote was split rather than unanimous, which would not have been possible if the Garfield language only applied to the unit rule.

The next serious challenge to the freedom of Republican National Convention delegates to vote their consciences came from state laws purporting to bind delegates to the outcome of state primaries. The first primaries affecting delegates to the convention occurred in 1912, and the first delegation to directly ignore a state law that sought to bind delegates was Oregon's in 1912.[3] Oregon subsequently ignored the primary results at the 1916 and 1920 conventions as well, and in two of the three instances the secretary of the convention polled the delegation and recorded the votes as the delegates wished, with complete disregard for Oregon's law instructing them how to vote. At the 1916 convention, no effort was made to enforce the binding so no poll of the delegation was even needed.

Throughout the next several decades, delegates continued to assert on the convention floor their right to vote as their conscience and judgment dictated, and have their vote recorded as they wished. Despite this extensive history – plus a pair of Supreme Court rulings indicating that binding of delegates by state law was unconstitutional – the campaign of President Gerald Ford managed to add language to the 1976 convention rules that for the first time recognized and enforced binding according to state laws, part of their strategy to deny Ronald Reagan the nomination.

The 1980 convention promptly removed that language, and what is now Rule 37 (b) of the temporary rules of the 2016 convention is little changed in language, intent or application from either the 1880 rule authored by Garfield or the 1980 rule restored by the Reagan campaign.

The inescapable conclusion from this history is this: As long as the 2016 Republican National Convention includes the language of Rule 37(b) in more or less identical form, every delegate arriving in Cleveland is free to vote his or her conscience in any and all matters that require a

> **As long as the 2016 Republican National Convention includes the language of Rule 37(b) in more or less identical form, every delegate arriving in Cleveland is free to vote his or her conscience on the first ballot for the presidential nomination.**

roll call of the states, including the first and any subsequent ballots for the presidential nomination.

As discussed in Chapter 6, this conclusion is not unanimously held – some have simply said this is a "selective reading" or that they have a "different interpretation" on the matter. As authors we make no claims of perfection, but simply ask two questions:

1. If our reading on the matter is selective, what readings have we overlooked? The official proceedings of nearly every Republican National Convention have been carefully reviewed, as well as the transcripts of several rules committee meetings. In addition, numerous academic papers, court decisions, media accounts, and books on the subject have been consulted as well. Those who may argue we have somehow been selective in our sources ought to bear the burden of providing the omitted materials.

2. If there is a different interpretation, on what is it based? The interpretation offered here is based on the text of the rule, the original intent of the rule, and an extensive and consistent history of precedents describing numerous occasions when the interpretation offered here was applied. A different interpretation may be available under a doctrine of "living, breathing convention rules" similar to that applied by leftists to the U.S. Constitution. But even in the rewriting of the Constitution, liberal judges generally offer an explanation of how they believe the plain text has evolved into something else in order to meet progressive sensibilities, and it should be similarly expected from those saying they have a different interpretation to explain on what grounds that conclusion is based.

Some questioning the conclusions, or at least the desirability of the conclusions, may wonder about the purpose of this book, and our aim in making this argument. The book is not, as has been alleged by some even before publication, intended to help or hinder any specific candidate. Instead, the authors' goal is primarily to impress upon delegates to the 2016 Republican National Convention that they are the ultimate power in the Republican Party, and that this power is to be jealously guarded against intrusions.

The Republican Party is a private organization, and it has a specific structure, process and hierarchy that gives it its legitimacy. Delegates to the national convention are far more than observers who come to the host city for free food, sightseeing, and enjoyment of the speeches and spectacle that make up the convention. Most are elected through a process that begins at local precinct meetings or county conventions, and their role at the national convention is to represent to the best of their ability the interests, perspectives, and priorities of their fellow Republicans at home, and to authorize and establish the policies and priorities of the national party for the next four years.

This is a monumental responsibility and is not to be casually neglected or given away to others. Just as we would expect Congress to resist any effort by the president to strip the body of its powers and turn the institution into a ceremonial body, Republican delegates should similarly resist efforts by others to intrude on their power.

These intrusions can take many forms. The binding of delegates to the Republican National Convention under state law is the most obvious danger to the power of delegates. After all, if a state can require delegates to vote for a specific candidate for president, might they be able to require them to vote for a specific candidate for vice president? This is not farfetched – in 1916 the Oregon primary ballot included a candidate for vice president for whom the delegation was ostensibly bound to vote (they largely ignored the instruction).

Binding delegates raises the question of what all they can be bound on. At the hotly contested 1912 convention pitting incumbent President William Taft against former President Theodore Roosevelt, some delegations announced they felt bound to vote in line with their preferred candidate's wishes and instructions, including credentials fights and the

rules of the convention itself. Allowing delegates to be bound raises the possibility that delegates could be forced to vote according to a specific candidate's instructions on all matters, including the platform.

And in an age when the progressive left is seeking to make it functionally illegal to hold or at least express certain opinions, there is additional danger for the Republican Party. If delegates can be bound by state law to the results of a primary, then what would stop a state legislature from allowing platform positions to be voted on in a primary, with delegates bound to vote according to the outcome? It isn't difficult to see delegates being bound to vote against a platform plank protecting traditional marriage, or required to support massive global warming taxes and regulations, to cite just two examples where the progressive left is seeking to criminalize dissent.

Republicans who have been nominated for or elected to public office can also intrude on the power and authority of delegates, such as attempting to direct that rules be changed to benefit their own interests. Clearly the Ford campaign in 1976 wasn't interested in what was best for the party when it pushed through the Justice Amendment; it was simply trying to win the nomination. It also seems likely that the Romney campaign's successful push to revise the rules relating to who could be officially nominated was aimed at minimizing potential embarrassment, not furthering the interests of the party.

Candidates in recent years have also sought to select delegates from states or have delegates removed based on how loyal they are to the candidate, ignoring the wishes of Republican voters on who they want to send to the national convention to represent them.

And party officials including the Republican National Committee can also intrude on the power and authority of delegates to the national convention. One such obvious intrusion is the adoption of Rule 16(a) by the Republican National Committee following the 2012 convention, which (ineffectively) seeks to reduce delegates to mere spectators in the nomination of the party's presidential candidate by directing the secretary of the convention to record votes according to primary results instead of how delegates actually vote.

Delegates to the Republican National Convention are the ultimate authority for the national party, providing guidance and direction for the

four years between the end of one convention and the start of the next. They create the Republican National Committee anew each time, and the committee is subordinate to the convention. Allowing anyone – whether the state, candidates, or party officials – to intrude on this power threatens to upend the party, changing it from an organization run by grassroots citizens brought together by common interests to a top-down entity issuing orders from headquarters for subordinates to follow, or worse, an agency of the state answering not to Republicans but to government officials and bureaucrats.

> **Allowing anyone – whether the state, candidates, or party officials – to intrude on delegates' freedom to vote their conscience threatens to upend the party, changing it from an organization run by grassroots citizens brought together by common interests to a top-down entity issuing orders from headquarters for subordinates to follow.**

In order to have her vote recorded as she wishes, a delegate must stand up and assert that right on the floor of the convention – if she declines to assert it, then her vote is lost to her. Similarly, if delegates decline to stand up and assert their position as the ultimate power and authority of the Republican Party, the party will be lost to them. It is the authors' sincere hope that delegates to the 2016 Republican National Convention will retain the full power and authority they have customarily held since the opening of the first convention in 1856.

---

[1] Proceedings of the First Three Republican National Conventions, 21.

[2] Past conventions and presumably the 2016 convention as well are governed by the rules of the U.S. House of Representatives, except in case of conflict with the standing rules of the convention. Sec. 5 of Rule I of the U.S. House of Representatives states, "The Speaker shall decide all questions of order, subject to appeal by a Member, Delegate, or Resident Commissioner." See also "Points of Order, Rulings, and Appeals in the House of Representatives" by Congressional Research Service, 2006.

[3] Illinois might also lay claim to being the first to ignore primary instructions, although the Illinois delegates were elected directly by congressional district and the few votes for Taft may have been in accordance with those district instructions. The announcement of the delegation chair suggests confusion over how they were to vote rather than a desire to ignore the primary results. See Proceedings of the 1912 Republican National Convention, 391-392.

Appendix A –
Guidelines for Invoking Rule 37 & Rule 38

The following is based upon an extensive review and analysis of nearly 200 instances in past Republican conventions in which individual delegates have invoked the conscience protections embedded in what is now Rule 37 and Rule 38. These guidelines apply to any and all matters in which a roll call of the states is ordered, including committee reports, motions to adjourn or suspend the rules, and the Presidential and Vice-Presidential nominations.

1. Every delegate has the right to cast their vote according to their own judgment, preference, and conscience, without regard to any pledge, binding, instruction, or other restraint that might purport to be in place as a result of custom, state party rules, state law, ruling of the chair, or any other authority.

2. Any delegate has the right to challenge the vote announced by the delegation chairman.

3. Only seated delegates may announce a challenge – alternates may not, unless they are properly designated as voting in the place of a specific delegate.

4. The delegate must state a belief that the vote announced by the delegation chairman is in error.

5. Upon the statement of a challenge, no debate, discussion, explanation, or questioning is in order – the convention chair is to immediately order a poll of the delegation.

6. The challenge can only be raised after the vote has been announced – raising a challenge prior to the announcement of the vote can be ruled out of order.

7. The challenge must be given immediately following the announce-ment of the vote – raising the challenge after the roll call has moved on to another state can be ruled out of order, as will any challenge given at the conclusion of the roll call but prior to the announcement of the result.

8. The convention chair will not order a polling of the delegation because the delegation chairman indicates or even directly states the announced vote differs from the actual votes of delegates, or is being announced in accordance with the unit rule – a delegate *must* state a challenge to the announced vote before the chair will order a polling of the delegation.

9. A delegate can only challenge the correctness of the announced vote from their own delegation, not any other state.

The following language is suggested for invoking delegate conscience protections:

> Mr./Madame Chair, I challenge the correctness of the vote as announced by the delegation chair. I request a poll of the delegation under Rule 37(b).

Appendix B –
Evolution of the Republican Party's Delegate Conscience Protections

The following traces the evolution of the conscience protections embedded in the rules of the Republican National Convention.

1856: The first Republican convention

"That in voting for a candidate for President, the states be called in their order, and that the chairman of each delegation present the number of votes given to each candidate for President by the delegates from his state…"[1]

1876: Before the Garfield language of 1880 (two separate rules)

Rule 2: Each state shall be entitled to double the number of its senators and representatives in congress, according to the late apportionment, and each territory and the District of Columbia shall be entitled to two votes. The votes of each delegation shall be reported by its chairman.
Rule 6: In the record of votes by states, the vote of each state, territory, and the District of Columbia shall be announced by the chairman; and, in case the vote of any state, territory, or the District of Columbia shall be divided, the chairman shall announce the number of votes cast for any candidate, or for or against any proposition.[2]

1880: The Garfield language

Rule 8: In the record of the vote by States, the vote of each State, territory, and the District of Columbia shall be announced by the chairman; and in case the vote of any State, territory, or District of Columbia shall be divided, the chairman shall announce the number of votes cast for any candidate, or for or against any proposition; but if exception is taken by any delegate to the correct-

ness of such announcement by the chairman of his delegation, the President of the Convention shall direct the roll of members of such delegation to be called, and the result shall be recorded with the votes individually given.[3]

1964: **Explicit unit rule prohibition added**

Rule 18 (a): In the balloting, the vote of each State shall be announced by the Chairman of the respective Delegations; and in case the vote of any State shall be divided, the Chairman shall announce the number of votes for each candidate, or for or against any proposition; but if exception is taken by any Delegate to the correctness of such announcement by the Chairman of his Delegation, the Chairman of the Convention shall direct the roll of members of such Delegation to be called and the result shall be recorded in accordance with the vote of the several Delegates in such Delegation. No Delegate or Alternate shall be bound by any attempt of any State or Congressional District, the District of Columbia, Puerto Rico or the Virgin Islands to impose the unit rule.[4]

1976: **"Justice amendment" added to enforce binding by 19 states**

Rule 18 (a): In the balloting, the vote of each State shall be announced by the chairman of the respective delegations; and in case the vote of any state shall be divided, the chairman shall announce the number of votes for each candidate, or for or against any proposition; but if exception is taken by an delegate to the correctness of such announcement by the chairman of that delegation, the chairman of the convention shall direct the roll of members of such delegation to be called and the result shall be recorded in accordance with the vote of the several delegates in such delegation; provided, however, that in any event, the vote of each state for the nomination for President shall be announced and recorded (or in the absence of an announcement shall be recorded) in accordance with the results of any binding Presidential primary or direct election of delegates bound or pledged pursuant to state law. No

delegate or alternate shall be bound by any attempt of any state or Congressional district, to impose the unit rule.[5]

2012: Most recent, and current temporary rule for 2016 convention

Rule 37 (b): In the balloting, the vote of each state shall be announced by the chairman of each state's delegation, or his or her designee; and in case the vote of any state shall be divided, the chairman shall announce the number of votes for each candidate, or for or against any proposition; but if exception is taken by any delegate from that state to the correctness of such announcement by the chairman of that delegation, the chairman of the convention shall direct the roll of members of such delegation to be called, and then shall report back the result to the convention at the conclusion of the balloting by the other states. The result shall be recorded in accordance with the vote of the several delegates in such delegation.

Rule 38: No delegate or alternate delegate shall be bound by any attempt of any State or Congressional district to impose the unit rule. A "unit rule" prohibited by this section means a rule or law under with a delegation at the national convention casts its entire vote as a unite as determined by a majority vote of the delegation.[6]

[1] Proceedings of the First Three Republican Conventions, Republican National Convention (1893), p. 27,

[2] Proceedings of the 1876 Republican National Convention, pp. 34 - 35

[3] Proceedings of the 1880 Republican National Convention, p. 43

[4] Proceedings of the 1964 Republican National Convention, p. 158

[5] Proceedings of the 1976 Republican National Convention, pp. 260 - 261

[6] The Rules of the Republican Party, as adopted by the 2012 Republican National Convention and amended by the Republican National Committee on April 12, 2013, January 24, 2014, May 9, 2014, and August 8, 2014

Appendix C –
Conscience Protection Invocations

Page in Proceedings	Convention Year	State Delegation	Question
71	1860	Maryland	presidential nomination
*	1868	Pennsylvania	vice presidential nomination
*	1868	Pennsylvania	vice presidential nomination
*	1868	Pennsylvania	vice presidential nomination
88	1876	Pennsylvania	presidential nomination
99	1876	Pennsylvania	chair's ruling
32	1880	Alabama	committee directions
33	1880	Kentucky	committee directions
199	1880	New York	presidential nomination
203	1880	Florida	presidential nomination
204	1880	West Virginia	presidential nomination
219	1880	Virginia	presidential nomination
253	1880	Alabama	presidential nomination
256	1880	Virginia	presidential nomination
258	1880	West Virginia	presidential nomination
261	1880	Minnesota	presidential nomination
263	1880	Alabama	presidential nomination
272	1880	Maryland	presidential nomination
272	1880	Minnesota	presidential nomination
273	1880	Mississippi	presidential nomination
274	1880	Nevada	presidential nomination
274	1880	South Carolina	presidential nomination
275	1880	Tennessee	presidential nomination
276	1880	Virginia	presidential nomination
130	1884	New York	adjournment
131	1884	Pennsylvania	adjournment
132	1884	DC	adjournment
138	1884	Arkansas	presidential nomination
139	1884	Florida	presidential nomination
139	1884	Kansas	presidential nomination

* The 1868 invocatons of conscience protections are not recorded in the official proceedings, but have been verified as occuring through multiple historical sources and references.

Page in Proceedings	Convention Year	State Delegation	Question
140	1884	DC	presidential nomination
140	1884	Louisiana	presidential nomination
142	1884	Alabama	presidential nomination
143	1884	Arkansas	presidential nomination
144	1884	Florida	presidential nomination
144	1884	Illinois	presidential nomination
144	1884	Indiana	presidential nomination
145	1884	Kentucky	presidential nomination
145	1884	Louisiana	presidential nomination
145	1884	Missouri	presidential nomination
146	1884	DC	presidential nomination
146	1884	New York	presidential nomination
148	1884	Pennsylvania	presidential nomination
148	1884	Massachusetts	presidential nomination
148	1884	Texas	presidential nomination
153	1884	Illinois	adjournment
153	1884	New York	adjournment
154	1884	North Carolina	adjournment
154	1884	Pennsylvania	adjournment
154	1884	Tennessee	adjournment
156	1884	Florida	presidential nomination
157	1884	Illinois	presidential nomination
158	1884	Kentucky	presidential nomination
158	1884	Louisiana	presidential nomination
159	1884	Massachusetts	presidential nomination
159	1884	New York	presidential nomination
160	1884	North Carolina	presidential nomination
160	1884	South Carolina	presidential nomination
160	1884	Tennessee	presidential nomination
161	1884	DC	presidential nomination
161	1884	Texas	presidential nomination
154	1888	Louisiana	presidential nomination
155	1888	Minnesota	presidential nomination
156	1888	Pennsylvania	presidential nomination
156	1888	South Carolina	presidential nomination
157	1888	Tennessee	presidential nomination
158	1888	Virginia	presidential nomination

Page in Proceedings	Convention Year	State Delegation	Question
161	1888	Kentucky	presidential nomination
161	1888	South Carolina	presidential nomination
162	1888	Virginia	presidential nomination
164	1888	Texas	presidential nomination
164	1888	Georgia	presidential nomination
164	1888	Pennsylvania	presidential nomination
165	1888	Virginia	presidential nomination
169	1888	New York	adjournment
174	1888	New York	presidential nomination
175	1888	North Carolina	presidential nomination
176	1888	Virginia	presidential nomination
179	1888	Virginia	presidential nomination
188	1888	Ohio	presidential nomination
189	1888	Tennessee	presidential nomination
189	1888	Virginia	presidential nomination
191	1888	Pennsylvania	presidential nomination
191	1888	California	presidential nomination
194	1888	Alabama	presidential nomination
195	1888	Kansas	presidential nomination
195	1888	Kentucky	presidential nomination
196	1888	North Carolina	presidential nomination
197	1888	South Carolina	presidential nomination
197	1888	Tennessee	presidential nomination
198	1888	Virginia	presidential nomination
231	1888	Virginia	vice presidential nomination
73	1892	Illinois	credentials
74	1892	Louisiana	credentials
77	1892	New York	credentials
78	1892	North Carolina	credentials
79	1892	Texas	credentials
84	1892	Connecticut	credentials
135	1892	California	presidential nomination
135	1892	Illinois	presidential nomination
136	1892	North Carolina	presidential nomination
137	1892	Ohio	presidential nomination
138	1892	Pennsylvania	presidential nomination
139	1892	South Carolina	presidential nomination

Page in Proceedings	Convention Year	State Delegation	Question
91	1896	California	platform
92	1896	Illinois	platform
92	1896	Kansas	platform
93	1896	Missouri	platform
93	1896	North Carolina	platform
93	1896	South Dakota	platform
94	1896	Tennessee	platform
94	1896	Virginia	platform
94	1896	New Mexico	platform
96	1896	Iowa	platform
97	1896	Kansas	platform
97	1896	New Mexico	platform
97	1896	Virginia	platform
124	1896	Florida	presidential nomination
124	1896	Georgia	presidential nomination
124	1896	Alabama	presidential nomination
125	1896	Illinois	presidential nomination
125	1896	Mississippi	presidential nomination
126	1896	Montana	presidential nomination
126	1896	New York	presidential nomination
127	1896	Texas	presidential nomination
127	1896	Virginia	presidential nomination
127	1896	New Mexico	presidential nomination
130	1904	Illinois	rules
180	1908	New York	presidential nomination
181	1908	South Carolina	presidential nomination
58	1912	Pennsylvania	temporary chair
146	1912	Arkansas	credentials
147	1912	California	credentials
148	1912	Georgia	credentials
148	1912	Indiana	credentials
149	1912	Kentucky	credentials
151	1912	New York	credentials
154	1912	North Carolina	credentials
155	1912	Oregon	credentials
155	1912	Pennsylvania	credentials
158	1912	Texas	credentials

Page in Proceedings	Convention Year	State Delegation	Question
180	1912	California	credentials
181	1912	Indiana	credentials
181	1912	Maryland	credentials
182	1912	New York	credentials
184	1912	North Carolina	credentials
184	1912	Oregon	credentials
187	1912	Maryland	credentials
188	1912	Massachusetts	credentials
188	1912	Oregon	credentials
195	1912	Maryland	credentials
213	1912	Massachusetts	credentials
214	1912	New York	credentials
216	1912	Pennsylvania	credentials
366	1912	California	platform
367	1912	Maryland	platform
367	1912	Illinois	platform
369	1912	North Carolina	platform
370	1912	Massachusetts	platform
391	1912	California	presidential nomination
391	1912	Illinois	presidential nomination
393	1912	Maryland	presidential nomination
394	1912	Massachusetts	presidential nomination
400	1912	Oregon	presidential nomination
401	1912	South Carolina	presidential nomination
404	1912	Illinois	vice presidential nomination
112	1916	Arizona	nominations
175	1916	New York	presidential nomination
179	1916	Pennsylvania	presidential nomination
185	1916	Massachusetts	presidential nomination
210	1916	Oregon	vice presidential nomination
92	1920	Georgia	national committeeman
183	1920	Oregon	presidential nomination
186	1920	Georgia	presidential nomination
186	1920	North Carolina	presidential nomination
189	1920	Oregon	presidential nomination
199	1920	Ohio	presidential nomination
199	1920	Oregon	presidential nomination

Page in Proceedings	Convention Year	State Delegation	Question
202	1920	Georgia	presidential nomination
203	1920	Michigan	presidential nomination
204	1920	Ohio	presidential nomination
207	1920	Florida	presidential nomination
207	1920	Michigan	presidential nomination
209	1920	Texas	presidential nomination
215	1920	Michigan	presidential nomination
216	1920	Oklahoma	presidential nomination
218	1920	Texas	presidential nomination
221	1920	Maryland	presidential nomination
229	1920	California	vice presidential nomination
66	1928	Georgia	credentials
174	1928	South Carolina	platform
216	1928	Georgia	presidential nomination
280	1940	Georgia	presidential nomination
286	1940	Georgia	presidential nomination
290	1940	Georgia	presidential nomination
292	1940	Maryland	presidential nomination
292	1940	New York	presidential nomination
295	1940	Florida	presidential nomination
298	1940	California	presidential nomination
298	1940	Oregon	presidential nomination
303	1940	Oklahoma	presidential nomination
305	1940	Iowa	presidential nomination
307	1940	California	presidential nomination
312	1940	Oregon	presidential nomination
314	1940	Washington	presidential nomination
315	1940	Wisconsin	presidential nomination
259	1948	Maine	presidential nomination
260	1948	Wisconsin	presidential nomination
263	1948	Michigan	presidential nomination
264	1948	Nebraska	presidential nomination
265	1948	Ohio	presidential nomination
267	1948	Texas	presidential nomination
268	1948	Wisconsin	presidential nomination
270	1948	Connecticut	presidential nomination
273	1948	California	presidential nomination

Page in Proceedings	Convention Year	State Delegation	Question
48	1952	New Jersey	rules
50	1952	Wisconsin	rules
51	1952	Puerto Rico	rules
185	1952	Indiana	credentials
186	1952	Maryland	credentials
187	1952	New York	credentials
190	1952	Pennsylvania	credentials
192	1952	Rhode Island	credentials
192	1952	Virginia	credentials
193	1952	Puerto Rico	credentials
389	1952	Florida	presidential nomination
390	1952	Iowa	presidential nomination
392	1952	Missouri	presidential nomination
393	1952	Nebraska	presidential nomination
395	1952	New Mexico	presidential nomination
396	1952	South Carolina	presidential nomination
397	1952	Virginia	presidential nomination
398	1952	Wyoming	presidential nomination
358	1964	Florida	presidential nomination
372	1968	New Jersey	presidential nomination
375	1968	Virginia	presidential nomination
376	1968	Virgin Islands	presidential nomination
427	1968	Utah	vice presidential nomination
254	1976	New Jersey	rules
418	1976	Virginia	presidential nomination
444	1976	Alabama	vice presidential nomination

About the Authors

Curly Haugland currently serves as the Republican National Committeeman from North Dakota, a position he has held since 2004. He has served on the Rules Committee of both the Republican National Convention and the Republican National Committee. Prior to becoming a national committeeman he served as Chairman of the North Dakota Republican Party.

Haugland is also a successful businessman, starting and continuing to run a swimming pool supply company headquartered in North Dakota. He and his wife Darlene have three children.

Sean Parnell is a public policy consultant residing in Virginia, working primarily for think tanks and advocacy organizations with a free-market, limited-government orientation. He previously was the president of the Center for Competitive Politics and vice-president at The Heartland Institute.

Parnell also is the author of the book *The Self-Pay Patient: Affordable Healthcare in the Age of Obamacare*. He lives in Virginia with his wife Anne and their son.

About the Publisher –
Citizens in Charge Foundation

In publishing *Unbound: The Conscience of a Republican Delegate* by Curly Haugland and Sean Parnell, Citizens in Charge Foundation hopes to enhance the debate about the roles political parties have historically played in our political discourse, the rights of citizens to form political parties, and the authority political parties and, more specifically, party delegates have in nominating a presidential candidate.

Citizens in Charge Foundation is a not-for-profit and non-partisan charitable foundation working, through education and litigation, to ensure citizens understand their rights within the political process and are fully in charge of their government.

The foundation seeks to protect the First Amendment rights to speak, assemble, to petition and to freely associate so that citizens can advance their political beliefs. Most often, Citizens in Charge Foundation addresses the challenges to citizen participation in so-called "direct" democracy: initiatives, referendums and recall petitions. But citizens have an equal right, and need, to engage in nominating and choosing their elected officials through the ability to vote their conscience so as to make representative democracy truly "representative."

13168 Centerpointe Way
Suite 202
Woodbridge, Virginia 22193

www.CitizensinChargeFoundation.org

www.ingramcontent.com/pod-product-compliance
Lightning Source LLC
Chambersburg PA
CBHW071201280526
45787CB00002B/567